Poets in Hand

A Puffin Quintet

Charles Causley

John Fuller

Elizabeth Jennings

Vernon Scannell

John Walsh

Chosen and introduced by Anne Harvey

 Puffin Books

Puffin Books, Penguin Books Ltd, Harmondsworth, Middlesex, England
Viking Penguin Inc., 40 West 23rd Street, New York, New York 10010, U.S.A.
Penguin Books Australia Ltd, Ringwood, Victoria, Australia
Penguin Books Canada Ltd, 2801 John Street, Markham, Ontario, Canada L3R 1B4
Penguin Books (N.Z.) Ltd, 182–190 Wairau Road, Auckland 10, New Zealand

This collection first published 1985
Reprinted 1986, 1987

Introductory material and collection copyright © Anne Harvey, 1985
Illustrations copyright © Christine Thwaites, 1985
All rights reserved

Made and printed in Great Britain by
Richard Clay Ltd, Bungay, Suffolk
Filmset in Monophoto Photina

To the memory of Eleanor Farjeon

Contents

Acknowledgements

I should like to thank all those who have been so co-operative over the preparation of this anthology: Mary Walsh for her generous help with her husband's work and for allowing us to use some unpublished poems; Charles Causley, John Fuller, Elizabeth Jennings and Vernon Scannell, who have shown great interest and given much encouragement, and Novello and Company Ltd for permission to include John Fuller's *Half a Fortnight* and *Lullaby*.

Charles Causley

Charles Causley was born in Launceston, Cornwall, in August 1917, and educated at Launceston National School, Horwell Grammar School, Launceston College and Peterborough Training College. He served in the Royal Navy from 1940 to 1946, then taught in Cornwall from 1947 to 1976. He was Honorary Visiting Fellow in Poetry at the University of Exeter in 1973/4, and a member of the Arts Council Literature Panel from 1962 to 1966. He was awarded Society of Authors' Travelling Scholarships in 1954 and 1966, the Queen's Gold Medal for Poetry in 1967, and a Cholmondeley Award in 1971. In 1958 he was made a Fellow of the Royal Society of Literature. He received his Honorary D.Litt (University of Exeter) in 1977.

His published work includes *Union Street* (1957) and *Johnny Alleluia* (1961), both published by Hart-Davis; *Underneath the Water* (1968), *Figure of 8* (1969), *Collected Poems* (1975), *The Animals' Carol* (1978), and *Secret Destinations* (1984), all published by Macmillan; *Figgie Hobbin* (Macmillan, 1970; Puffin, 1979); and the plays *The Ballad of Aucassin and Nicolette* (Kestrel, 1976) and *The Gift of a Lamb* (Robson, 1978; Puffin, 1980). He is editor of *The Puffin Book of Magic Verse* (1974), *The Puffin Book of Salt-Sea Verse* (1978) and *The Sun, Dancing* (Kestrel, 1983; Puffin, 1984).

Poems in the following collection are taken from *The Ballad of Aucassin and Nicolette*, *Collected Poems*, *Figgie Hobbin*, *Figure of 8*, *Johnny Alleluia*, *Secret Destinations*, *Underneath the Water*, *Union Street*, and *Stories in Verse for Children* (Batsford).

Charles Causley still lives in Launceston, a small market town in North Cornwall, where he was born. His first school, where he himself later became a teacher, was the local National School, described by him as 'a huge, booming, granite-and-slate building stranded like an ark on the edge of the borough allotments. It had been put up in 1840 and looked it: the name and date over the front door had begun to crumble long before I first attended there in the 1920s.'

He remembers hearing little poetry until he was about eleven, but read any prose he could get hold of. Dickens's *David Copperfield* was one of his favourite stories, and he was deeply affected by the passage where little Em'ly says of the sea: 'Ah! but it's cruel. I have seen it tear a boat as big as our house all to pieces.'

As a child in Cornwall, where no one can live far from the ocean, the sea made an early impression on him; he was fearful of it and fascinated by it. Both emotions come into his writing. As a small boy he had no idea that one day he would edit *The Puffin Book of Salt-Sea Verse*.

On Sunday evenings his mother would take him to the tiny church of St Thomas the Apostle, and sometimes they would sing 'Now the Day is Over', a hymn written by the Reverend Sabine Baring-Gould (later to be the subject of one of his poems). When they reached the lines

> Guard the sailors tossing
> On the deep blue sea ...

the small Charles always imagined the church gave a ship-like lurch.

Beside this church ran a tributary of the River Tamar, known locally at this point as St Thomas River, or Water. And 'By St Thomas Water' was the poem that first led me to Charles Causley's writing; it haunts me still. I felt it must be true, and was interested when he told me that it was based on an incident in the childhood of himself and a friend. It is this haunting quality that runs through many of his poems. They are very rhythmic, often ballad-like, the lines move, the words are vivid. Many questions are asked:

> Quiet stone, cautious stone,
> What do you tell me now?

and ...

> Who is that child I see wandering, wandering ...?
> Where does he come from, and what is his name?

Some begin in a light-hearted manner but by the end you're thinking a little harder, there's a shudder up your spine, goose-pimples along your arm ...

As a schoolboy Charles Causley only wrote poems when told to, and was surprised when the results brought praise. He was hypnotized by the sound of words.

In the 1930s there was a big unemployment problem, and any job was worth hanging on to. Even so, he found being a clerk in a building company 'stupefyingly boring'. Reading became an escape. Before long he discovered poets like W. H. Auden, Cecil Day-Lewis, Louis MacNeice, Stephen Spender and T. S. Eliot. Then the First World War poets; on his first holiday in London he picked up a second-hand edition of Siegfried Sassoon's war poems in a bookshop. For the first time he wanted to learn poetry by heart.

By 1940 there was war, and Charles Causley joined the Navy. Leaving home was a shock, and he was home-sick and seasick. But the jargon of the sailors left him spellbound. 'Grab-hooks' were fingers; 'stagger-juice' meant rum; 'stroppy' was argumentative; 'in the rattle' meant you were in trouble. Ideas moved around his head as he worked; the Navy gave him his first subjects for poems ... separation, death, loss, odd characters.

Causley is also a musician. As a teenager he played the piano in a local group, and while a teacher always trained and conducted the school choir. After many years of teaching he resigned in order to write full-time. Now he travels a good deal, but always returns to Cornwall; the countryside, sea, places, people, legends are part of his life. As well as being one of our most popular poets, he broadcasts and gives readings of his poetry. I like listening to him; he's always himself, and manages to capture the mood exactly while remaining relaxed and natural.

Many poetry-writing years have taught him that poetry is right there, under one's very nose, waiting to be gathered; also that poets choose words with far more care than most people imagine. 'They are as important, say, as selecting one's own individual teeth.'

Who?

Who is that child I see wandering, wandering
Down by the side of the quivering stream?
Why does he seem not to hear, though I call to him?
Where does he come from, and what is his name?

Why do I see him at sunrise and sunset
Taking, in old-fashioned clothes, the same track?
Why, when he walks, does he cast not a shadow
Though the sun rises and falls at his back?

Why does the dust lie so thick on the hedgerow
By the great field where a horse pulls the plough?
Why do I see only meadows, where houses
Stand in a line by the riverside now?

Why does he move like a wraith by the water,
Soft as the thistledown on the breeze blown?
When I draw near him so that I may hear him,
Why does he say that his name is my own?

On the Border

By the window-drizzling leaves,
Underneath the rain's shadow,
'What is that land,' you said, 'beyond
Where the river bends the meadow?

'Is it Cornwall? Is it Devon?
Those promised fields, blue as the vine,
Wavering under new-grown hills;
Are they yours, or mine?'

When day, like a crystal, broke
We saw what we could see.
No Man's Land was no man's land.
It was the sea.

Timothy Winters

Timothy Winters comes to school
With eyes as wide as a football pool,
Ears like bombs and teeth like splinters:
A blitz of a boy is Timothy Winters.

His belly is white, his neck is dark,
And his hair is an exclamation mark.
His clothes are enough to scare a crow
And through his britches the blue winds blow.

When teacher talks he won't hear a word
And he shoots down dead the arithmetic-bird,
He licks the patterns off his plate
And he's not even heard of the Welfare State.

Timothy Winters has bloody feet
And he lives in a house on Suez Street,
He sleeps in a sack on the kitchen floor
And they say there aren't boys like him any more.

Old Man Winters likes his beer
And his missus ran off with a bombardier,
Grandma sits in the grate with a gin
And Timothy's dosed with an aspirin.

The Welfare Worker lies awake
But the law's as tricky as a ten-foot snake,
So Timothy Winters drinks his cup
And slowly goes on growing up.

At Morning Prayers the Master helves
For children less fortunate than ourselves,
And the loudest response in the room is when
Timothy Winters roars 'Amen!'

So come one angel, come on ten:
Timothy Winters says 'Amen
Amen amen amen amen.'
Timothy Winters, Lord.
                                        Amen.

helves: a dialect word from North Cornwall used to describe the alarmed lowing of cattle (as when a cow is separated from her calf); a desperate, pleading note

On Being Asked to Write a School Hymn

Tune: Buckland
('Loving Shepherd of Thy Sheep')

On a starless night and still
Underneath a sleeping hill
Comes the cry of sheep and kine
From the slaughter house to mine.

Fearful is the call and near
That I do not want to hear,
Though it has been said by some
That the animal is dumb.

Gone the byre and gone the breeze
And the gently moving trees
As with stabbing eye they run
In a clear, electric sun.

Now, red-fingered to their trade
With the shot and with the blade,
Rubber-booted angels white
Enter as the morning light.

But who wields that knife and gun
Does not strike the blow alone,
And there is no place to stand
Other than at his right hand.

God, who does not dwell on high
In the wide, unwinking sky,
And whose quiet counsels start
Simply from the human heart,

Teach us strong and teach us true
What to say and what to do,
That we love as best we can
All Thy creatures. Even man.

Amen.

By St Thomas Water

By St Thomas Water
Where the river is thin
We looked for a jam-jar
To catch the quick fish in.
Through St Thomas Churchyard
Jessie and I ran
The day we took the jam-pot
Off the dead man.

On the scuffed tombstone
The grey flowers fell,
Cracked was the water,
Silent the shell.
The snake for an emblem
Swirled on the slab,
Across the beach of sky the sun
Crawled like a crab.

'If we walk,' said Jessie,
'Seven times round,
We shall hear a dead man
Speaking underground.'
Round the stone we danced, we sang,
Watched the sun drop,
Laid our heads and listened
At the tomb-top.

Soft as the thunder
At the storm's start
I heard a voice as clear as blood,

Strong as the heart.
But what words were spoken
I can never say,
I shut my fingers round my head,
Drove them away.

'What are those letters, Jessie,
Cut so sharp and trim
All round this holy stone
With earth up to the brim?'
Jessie traced the letters
Black as coffin-lead.
'He is not dead but sleeping,'
Slowly she said.

I looked at Jessie,
Jessie looked at me,
And our eyes in wonder
Grew wide as the sea.
Past the green and bending stones
We fled hand in hand,
Silent through the tongues of grass
To the river strand.

By the creaking cypress
We moved as soft as smoke
For fear all the people
Underneath awoke.
Over all the sleepers
We darted light as snow
In case they opened up their eyes,
Called us from below.

Many a day has faltered
Into many a year
Since the dead awoke and spoke
And we would not hear.
Waiting in the cold grass
Under a crinkled bough,
Quiet stone, cautious stone,
What do you tell me now?

Child's Song

Christopher Beer
   Used to live here,
Where the white water
   Winds over the weir,
Close to the claw
   Of the pawing sea,
Under the spear
   Of a cypress tree.

Never a nightingale
   Rings on the bough,
Burned is the orchard
   And broken the plough.
Out of the orient
   Light like a lash
Severed the sky
   And the river ran ash.

Over the valley
   Dawdled the fire
Swallowing city
   Steeple and spire,
All the proud people
   Nowhere to hide
Kindling flowers
   Of flame as they died.

Nobody passes
   Nor sheds a salt tear,
No one wears mourning
   For Christopher Beer:
Free as the fountain,
   Green as a gun,
Rich as the rainbow
   And blind as the sun.

Infant Song

Don't you love my baby, mam,
Lying in his little pram,

Polished all with water clean,
The finest baby ever seen?

    Daughter, daughter, if I could
    I'd love your baby as I should,

    But why the suit of signal red,
    The horns that grow out of his head,

    Why does he burn with brimstone heat,
    Have cloven hooves instead of feet,

    Fishing hooks upon each hand,
    The keenest tail that's in the land,

    Pointed ears and teeth so stark
    And eyes that flicker in the dark?

Don't you love my baby, mam?

    Dearest, I do not think I can.
    I do not, do not think I can.

The Reverend Sabine
Baring-Gould

The Reverend Sabine Baring-Gould (1834–1924)
was Rector for 43 years at Lewtrenchard in Devon. He is
the author of the hymn 'Onward, Christian Soldiers'.

The Reverend Sabine Baring-Gould,
    Rector (sometime) at Lew,
Once at a Christmas party asked,
    'Whose pretty child are you?'

(The Rector's family was long,
    His memory was poor,
And as to who was who had grown
    Increasingly unsure).

At this, the infant on the stair
    Most sorrowfully sighed.
'Whose pretty little girl am I?
    Why, *yours*, papa!' she cried.

Green Man in the Garden

Green man in the garden
    Staring from the tree,
Why do you look so long and hard
    Through the pane at me?

Your eyes are dark as holly,
    Of sycamore your horns,
Your bones are made of elder-branch,
    Your teeth are made of thorns.

Your hat is made of ivy-leaf,
    Of bark your dancing shoes,
And evergreen and green and green
    Your jacket and shirt and trews.

Leave your house and leave your land
    And throw away the key,
And never look behind, he creaked,
    And come and live with me.

I bolted up the window,
    I bolted up the door,
I drew the blind that I should find
    The green man never more.

But when I softly turned the stair
    As I went up to bed,
I saw the green man standing there.
    Sleep well, my friend, he said.

Green Man, Blue Man

As I was walking through Guildhall Square
I smiled to see a green man there,
But when I saw him coming near
My heart was filled with nameless fear.

As I was walking through Madford Lane
A blue man stood there in the rain.
I asked him in by my front-door,
For I'd seen a blue man before.

As I was walking through Landlake Wood
A grey man in the forest stood,
But when he turned and said, 'Good day'
I shook my head and ran away.

As I was walking by Church Stile
A purple man spoke there a while.
I spoke to him because, you see,
A purple man once lived by me.

But when the night falls dark and fell
How, O how, am I to tell,
Grey man, green man, purple, blue,
Which is which is which of you?

Miller's End

When we moved to Miller's End,
   Every afternoon at four
A thin shadow of a shade
   Quavered through the garden-door.

Dressed in black from top to toe
   And a veil about her head
To us all it seemed as though
   She came walking from the dead.

With a basket on her arm
   Through the hedge-gap she would pass,
Never a mark that we could spy
   On the flagstones or the grass.

When we told the garden-boy
   How we saw the phantom glide,
With a grin his face was bright
   As the pool he stood beside.

'That's no ghost-walk,' Billy said,
   'Nor a ghost you fear to stop –
Only old Miss Wickerby
   On a short cut to the shop.'

So next day we lay in wait,
   Passed a civil time of day,
Said how pleased we were she came
   Daily down our garden-way.

Suddenly her cheek it paled,
   Turned, as quick, from ice to flame.
'Tell me,' said Miss Wickerby.
   'Who spoke of me, and my name?'

'Bill the garden-boy.'
             She sighed,
   Said, 'Of course, you could not know
How he drowned – that very pool –
   A frozen winter – long ago.'

Tom Bone

My name is Tom Bone,
I live all alone
In a deep house on Winter Street.
  Through my mud wall
  The wolf-spiders crawl
  And the mole has his beat.

On my roof of green grass
All the day footsteps pass
In the heat and the cold,
  As snug in a bed
  With my name at its head
  One great secret I hold.

Tom Bone, when the owls rise
In the drifting night skies
Do you walk round about?
  All the solemn hours through
  I lie down just like you
  And sleep the night out.

Tom Bone, as you lie there
On your pillow of hair,
What grave thoughts do you keep?
  Tom says, 'Nonsense and stuff!
  You'll know soon enough,
  Sleep, darling, sleep.'

Riley

Down in the water-meadows Riley
Spread his wash on the bramble-thorn,
Sat, one foot in the moving water,
Bare as the day that he was born.

Candid was his curling whisker,
Brown his body as an old tree-limb,
Blue his eye as the jay above him
Watching him watch the minjies swim.

Four stout sticks for walls had Riley,
His roof was a rusty piece of tin,
As snug in the lew of a Cornish hedgerow
He watched the seasons out and in.

He paid no rates, he paid no taxes,
His lamp was the moon hung in the tree.
Though many an ache and pain had Riley
He envied neither you nor me.

Many a friend from bush or burrow
To Riley's hand would run or fly,
And soft he'd sing and sweet he'd whistle
Whatever the weather in the sky.

Till one winter's morning Riley
From the meadow vanished clean.
Gone was the rusty tin, the timber,
As if old Riley had never been.

What strange secret had old Riley?
Where did he come from? Where did he go?
Why was his heart as light as summer?
'Never know now,' said the jay. *'Never know.'*

minjies: small minnows
lew: lee

If You Should Go to Caistor Town

If you should go to Caistor town
    Where my true-love has gone,
Ask her why she went away
    And left me here alone.

She said the Caistor sky was blue,
    The wind was never cold,
The pavements were all made of pearl,
    The young were never old.

Never a word she told me more
    But when the year was fled,
Upon a bed of brightest earth
    She laid her gentle head.

When I went up to Caistor
    My suit was made of black,
And all her words like summer birds
    Upon the air came back.

O when I went to Caistor
    With ice the sky was sown,
And all the streets were chill and grey
    And they were made of stone.

John Polruddon

John Polruddon's house was on the cliff over
Pentewan, in south Cornwall. The story of his
disappearance dates from early Tudor times.

John Polruddon
All of a sudden
Went out of his house one night,

When a privateer
Came sailing near
Under his window-light.

They saw his jugs
His plates and mugs
His hearth as bright as brass,

His gews and gaws
And kicks and shaws
All through their spying-glass.

They saw his wine
His silver shine
They heard his fiddlers play.

'Tonight,' they said,
'Out of his bed
Polruddon we'll take away.'

And from a skiff
They climbed the cliff
And crossed the salt-wet lawn,

    And as they crept
    Polruddon slept
    The night away to dawn.

'In air or ground
What is that sound?'
Polruddon said, and stirred.

    They breathed, 'Be still,
    It was the shrill
    Of the scritch-owl you heard.'

'O yet again
I hear it plain,
But do I wake or dream?'

    'In morning's fog
    The otter-dog
    Is whistling by the stream.'

'Now from the sea
What comes for me
Beneath my window dark?'

    'Lie still, my dear,
    All that you hear
    Is the red fox's bark.'

Swift from his bed
Polruddon was sped
Before the day was white,

And head and feet
Wrapped in a sheet
They bore him down the height.

And never more
Through his own door
Polruddon went nor came,

Though many a tide
Has turned beside
The cliff that bears his name.

On stone and brick
Was ivy thick,
And the grey roof was thin,

And winter's gale
With fists of hail
Broke all the windows in.

The chimney-crown
It tumbled down
And up grew the green,

Till on the cliff
It was as if
A house had never been.

But when the moon
Swims late or soon
Across St Austell Bay,

What sight, what sound
Haunts air and ground
Where once Polruddon lay?

It is the high
White scritch-owl's cry,
The fox as dark as blood,

And on the hill
The otter still
Whistles beside the flood.

Billy Medals

Do you know Billy Medals
That warrior bold,
His stars made of silver,
His circles of gold?
O there don't seem a battle
Of land, sea or air
For fifty years past
But old Bill wasn't there.

He stands on the corner
As straight as a gun,
And his circles and stars
Catch the rays of the sun.
His stars and his circles
All glitter and gleam,
And just like the rainbow
His ribbons they beam.

You must know Billy Medals
With his chestful of gongs,
He knows all the war-stories
And all the war-songs.
His jacket is ragged,
His trousers are green,
And no one stands straighter
For 'God Save the Queen'.

Around his torn topper
Are badges in scores
Of goodness knows how many
Different corps.
But in war Billy Medals
Has never known harm
For he's never been farther
Than Fiveacre Farm.

When lads from the village
Dodged shrapnel and shell,
Billy Medals was cleaning out
Wishworthy Well.
When in deserts they sweated,
In oceans they froze,
Billy Medals was scaring
The rooks and the crows.

Did you see the brave soldier
New-home from the war
Give Billy the star
That once proudly he bore?
Billy Medals he cackled
And capered with glee
And the village-boys laughed,
But the soldier, not he.

Logs of Wood

When in the summer sky the sun
Hung like a golden ball,
John Willy from the Workhouse came
And loudly he would bawl:

Wood! Wood! Logs of wood
To keep out the cold!
Shan't be round tomorrow!
They all must be sold!

But O the sky was shining blue
And green was the spray.
It seemed as if the easy days
Would never pass away.

And when John Willy came to town
The laughter it would start,
And we would smile as he went by
Pushing his wooden cart.

John Willy, I can see you still,
Coming down Tower Street,
Your pointed nose, your cast-off clothes,
Your Charlie Chaplin feet.

And like the prophet you would stand
Calling loud and long,
But there were few who listened to
The story of your song.

Wood! Wood! Logs of wood
To keep out the cold!
Shan't be round tomorrow!
They all must be sold!

But now the snow is on the hill,
The ice is on the plain,
And dark as dark a shadow falls
Across my window-pane.

Tomorrow, ah, tomorrow –
That name I did not fear
Until Tomorrow came and said,
Good morrow. I am here.

Legend

Snow-blind the meadow; chiming ice
Struck at the wasted water's rim.
An infant in a stable lay.
A child watched for a sight of Him.

'I would have brought spring flowers,' she said.
'But where I wandered none did grow.'
Young Gabriel smiled, opened his hand,
And blossoms pierced the sudden snow.

She plucked the gold, the red, the green,
And with a garland entered in.
'What is your name?' Young Gabriel said.
The maid she answered, 'Magdalen.'

Mary, Mary Magdalene

On the east wall of the church of St Mary Magdalene at
Launceston in Cornwall is a granite figure of the saint. The
children of the town say that a stone lodged on her back
will bring good luck.

Mary, Mary Magdalene
Lying on the wall,
I throw a pebble on your back.
Will it lie or fall?

Send me down for Christmas
Some stockings and some hose,
And send before the winter's end
A brand-new suit of clothes.

Mary, Mary Magdalene
Under a stony tree,
I throw a pebble on your back.
What will you send me?

I'll send you for your christening
A woollen robe to wear,
A shiny cup from which to sup,
And a name to bear.

Mary, Mary Magdalene
Lying cool as snow,
What will you be sending me
When to school I go?

I'll send a pencil and a pen
That write both clean and neat,
And I'll send to the schoolmaster
A tongue that's kind and sweet.

Mary, Mary Magdalene
Lying in the sun,
What will you be sending me
Now I'm twenty-one?

I'll send you down a locket
As silver as your skin,
And I'll send you a lover
To fit a gold key in.

Mary, Mary Magdalene
Underneath the spray,
What will you be sending me
On my wedding-day?

I'll send you down some blossom,
Some ribbons and some lace,
And for the bride a veil to hide
The blushes on her face.

Mary, Mary Magdalene
Whiter than the swan,
Tell me what you'll send me,
Now my good man's dead and gone.

I'll send to you a single bed
On which you must lie,
And pillows bright where tears may light
That fall from your eye.

Mary, Mary Magdalene
Now nine months are done,
What will you be sending me
For my little son?

I'll send you for your baby
A lucky stone, and small,
To throw to Mary Magdalene
Lying on the wall.

The Obby Oss

The Obby Oss is a primitive figure carried by a dancer round the port
of Padstow, on the north coast of Cornwall, every year on 1 May to
herald the arrival of summer. It is accompanied by music, dancing, and
a great deal of merry-making. All the other festivals mentioned are also
still held in Cornwall: for instance, a chain of bonfires is lit throughout
the county on Midsummer Eve, the Eve of St John, since Midsummer
Day is also the feast of St John the Baptist.

When the Cornish say that they 'belong to' do something, they
mean that it is right and proper that something should be done: that it
is a personal responsibility.

Early one morning,
   Second of May,
Up jumped the Obby Oss,
   Said, 'I'm away!'

With his tall dunce-head
   And his canvas gown
He tiptoed the streets
   Of Padstow town.

The wild, wild ponies
   Of Bodmin Moor
Said, 'Go back, Obby,
   To Padstow shore!

'With your snappers of oak
   And your tail of horse
You can't come running
   On this race-course.'

He went to Helston,
   He jigged, he danced,
And in and out
   Of the houses pranced.

'You can't stop here,'
   They said, said they,
'If you won't dance the furry
   In the Helston way.'

He went to Brown Willy
   On the Eve of St John.
They said, 'Who's that
   With the black kilt on?

'You'll soon run, Obby,
   To your drinking-trough
When the midsummer fire
   Burns your top-knot off!'

He went to St Ives
   Where on the height
Danced ten pretty maids
   All dressed in white.

And round they ran
   To the fiddler's moan
In the waking light
   By John Knill's stone.

But, 'Obby!' they cried,
   'You must homeward blow!

Only ten pretty maids
    Round here may go.'

He went to St Columb
    For the hurling game.
'You must go back, Obby,
    From where you came!

'For high in the air
    Flies the silver ball,
And Obby can't catch
    Or kick at all.'

The County Council
    Gave a county stare,
Said, 'Who's that dancing
    With his legs all bare?

'Go back, Obby,
    To Padstow Bar
As quick as the light
    Of a shooting star.'

The people of Padstow
    Night and day
Watched for Obby
    Like the first of May.

Without old Obby
    And his dancing drum
They feared that the summer
    Never would come.

When April ended
    At the bell's first beat,
Obby came dancing
    Down the street.

'Welcome, Obby!'
    He heard them cheer,
'For we love you the best
    Of the Padstow year.'

'Never again
    Will I run or roam,'
Said Obby, 'from Padstow
    My own true home.

'See, the sun is rising,
    It dries up the dew,
That we may welcome summer
    As we belong to do.'

The Merrymaid

In Cornwall, a mermaid is called a merrymaid. The poet Robert
Stephen Hawker (1803–75) was Vicar of Morwenstow, on the north
coast of Cornwall, from 1834. His best-known ballad is 'And shall
Trelawny die?'

Robert Stephen Hawker,
Vicar of Morwenstow,
Dressed himself in a merrymaid skin,
Swam out with the flow.

And with a coral-branch he combed
His hair so limp and long,
And high in a screamy voice he sang
A sea-weedy sort of song.

From near and far the people came
To walk on the cliff-top green,
For none had heard a merrymaid sing
Nor ever a merrymaid seen.

The first night that the merrymaid sang
The moon was white as bone,
And sad was the song they heard her sing
As she sat on a slippery stone.

The second night that the merrymaid sang
The moon was beaming brass,
And sweet was the song they heard her sing
As she gazed in her looking-glass.

The third night that the merrymaid sang
The moon was thin and pale,
And when she had sung her sweet-sad song
She stood up straight on her tail.

As stiff as a soldier she stood up
In a phosphorescent sheen,
And with arms straight down by her sides she sang
'God Save our Gracious Queen.'

Then into the dancing sea she dove
To the running billows' roar,
And vanished beneath the wheeling waves
And was seen on the coast no more.

Robert Stephen Hawker,
Vicar of Morwenstow,
Stripped himself of the merrymaid skin
He wore from top to toe.

And the Vicar he smiled and pondered
As he went upstairs to bed
On the gullibility of man,
And sadly he shook his head.

A Sailor Sat on the Watery Shore

A sailor sat on the watery shore
   By the side of the shiny sea,
And as the billows railed and roared
   These words he said to me.
'I've sailed to the Rock from Plymouth Dock
   And from Sydney to Simonstown,
And oh but it's true that a life on the blue
   Ain't the same as the life on the brown.

'For there's gusts and there's gales and there's spirting
     whales
   And there's fish flying round like a fountain,
And there's bays and there's bights and there's Great
     Northern Lights,
   And there's oceans as deep as a mountain.
And then there's your mates in the varying states
   From the angel and saint to the sinner,
Though I think you will find they are much of a kind
   When you sit down beside 'em for dinner.

'And yarns by the fathom you'll hear 'em all spin
   Of ghost-ships and sea-serpents mighty,
Of mermaids divine, and of Crossing the Line
   With King Neptune and Queen Amphitrite.
O many the lays I could sing of the days
   As in suits dazzling white from the dhoby
We sauntered ashore in New York, Singapore,
   Or went up the line to Nairobi.

'And your eyes, my young friend, would jump out of your
      head,
   When the ship bade old England good-bye-ee,
At the antics of tars to the sound of guitars
   Whether strummed in Cadiz or Hawaii.
You may search the world through, but no friend is as true
   As the matelot so trim and stout-hearted,
Though when he comes on leave (and to tell it, I grieve)
   There's no man from his pay sooner parted.

'Furthermore,' said the sailor, 'it's certain to me
   As this beach is all covered with sand,
Though a sailor may find many sharks in the sea
   He will find even more on the land.'
'Ah, sailor,' I said, 'but I feel that your heart
   For the world of the wave is still yearning,
And I think I surmise from the look in your eyes
   That to it you'll soon be returning.'

'Good gracious!' the sailor said. 'Certainly not,
   And I can't think what gave you the notion
That once having left it, I'd wish to return
   To the dark, unpredictable ocean.
I've a nice little semi in Citadel Road
   That faces away from the sea,
And the reason it's thus – but, dear me, there's my bus
   And it's time for my afternoon tea!'

dhoby: the wash

[47]

My Mother Saw a Dancing Bear

My mother saw a dancing bear
By the schoolyard, a day in June.
The keeper stood with chain and bar
And whistle-pipe, and played a tune.

And bruin lifted up its head
And lifted up its dusty feet,
And all the children laughed to see
It caper in the summer heat.

They watched as for the Queen it died.
They watched it march. They watched it halt.
They heard the keeper as he cried,
'Now, roly-poly!' 'Somersault!'

And then, my mother said, there came
The keeper with a begging-cup,
The bear with burning coat of fur,
Shaming the laughter to a stop.

They paid a penny for the dance,
But what they saw was not the show;
Only, in bruin's aching eyes,
Far-distant forests, and the snow.

As I Went Down the Cat-walk

As I went down the cat-walk
  Where all the catkins blow,
I saw an old cat-burglar
  Beside a cattalo.
And O he miaowed and O he mewed
  Just like the cat-bird's call.
I said, 'Pray cease this catalogue
  Of scatty caterwaul.
I didn't catch your name, I fear,
  But how, my dear old chap,
Among such cataracts of tears
  May I take my cat-nap?'
He said, 'Of various cat-calls
  I'm running the gamut
Because upon my cat-fish
  No catsup has been put!
Such catchpenny behaviour
  It makes me ill, then iller.'
I said, 'Please don't excite yourself.
  Lean on this caterpillar.'
I plucked from off the apple tree
  A juicy, ripe cat's-head.
He took it with some cat-lap
  And felt much better fed.
And then he played cat's-cradle
  And turned cat in the pan,

And sailed to Catalonia
    All in a catamaran.
He sailed away by Catalan Bay
    That happy cataman.

cattalo: a cross between a buffalo and a cow
Catalan Bay: in Gibraltar

The Fiddler's Son

When I was a little lad
I lay within the cradle,
But through the living street I strolled
As soon as I was able.

There I met the King's young daughter,
She, too, walked the street.
'Come in, come in, little son of a fiddler.
Play me a tune sweet.'

It lasted scarcely a quarter of an hour.
The King he saw me singing.
'You rogue, you thief, what is that song
That to my child you're bringing?
In France there is a gallows built
Whereon you'll soon be swinging.'

In but the space of three short days
I had to climb the ladder.
'Oh give to me my fiddle to play,
For I'll not play hereafter.'

Then bowed I to, then bowed I fro,
On all the four strings telling.
A fine death lament played I,
And the King's tears were falling.

'My daughter is yours, little fiddler's son,
So to your bride come down.
In Austria is a castle built,
And you shall wear the crown.'

Anonymous, translated from the German

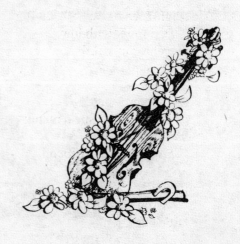

from the verse-play
The Ballad of Aucassin and Nicolette

THE LION AND THE LAMB

Tell you a story
   Old as Zion –
Pretty little lambkin
   Loved a lion.

Lion and lambkin –
   Man and wife?
Old man lion said,
   'Not on your life!

'High-born blood
   Don't mix with low;
She ain't upsettin'
   My *status quo*.'

Found her a cage
   Till her ways she'd mend;
Shut her away
   From her loving friend.

Painted the walls
   With fields and trees;
Little black lamb
   Didn't fancy these.

Round the cage
   A garden grew
Where roses blossomed
   And wild birds flew.

They sealed the door
   With an iron pin –
No way out
   And no way in.

Food for hunger,
   Drink for thirst,
But love was what
   She wanted most.

For company
   An old, old ewe
In case the lamb
   Herself she slew.

Now I've heard it says
   In the Book of Worth
That Heaven won't come
   Upon the earth,

And you won't lose sight
   Of the flames of Hell
Till lamb and lion
   Together dwell.

O you won't see a shine
   Of Heavenly weather
Till lion and lamb
   Lie down together;

And priest and prince
   And people agree
Of the Golden Age
   It's the golden key:

That lion and lamb
   Together lie down –
As long as it ain't
   In this here town.
   This here town,
   This here town.
As long as it ain't
   In this here town.

The Forest of Tangle

Deep in the Forest of Tangle
The King of the Makers sat
With a faggot of stripes for the tiger
And a flitter of wings for the bat.

He'd teeth and he'd claws for the cayman
And barks for the foxes and seals,
He'd a grindstone for sharpening swordfish
And electrical charges for eels.

He'd hundreds of kangaroo-pouches
On bushes and creepers and vines,
He'd hoots for the owls, and for glow-worms
He'd goodness knows how many shines.

He'd bellows for bullfrogs in dozens
And rattles for snakes by the score,
He'd hums for the humming-birds, buzzes for bees,
And elephant trumpets galore.

He'd pectoral fins for sea-fishes
With which they might glide through the air,
He'd porcupine quills and a bevy of bills
And various furs for the bear.

But O the old King of the Makers
With tears could have filled up a bay,
For no one had come to his warehouse
These many long years and a day.

And sadly the King of the Makers
His bits and his pieces he eyed
As he sat on a rock in the midst of his stock
And he cried and he cried and he cried.
He cried and he cried and he cried and he cried,
He cried and he cried and he cried.

Innocent's Song

Who's that knocking on the window,
Who's that standing at the door,
What are all those presents
Lying on the kitchen floor?

Who is the smiling stranger
With hair as white as gin,
What is he doing with the children
And who could have let him in?

Why has he rubies on his fingers,
A cold, cold crown on his head,
Why, when he caws his carol,
Does the salty snow run red?

Why does he ferry my fireside
As a spider on a thread,
His fingers made of fuses
And his tongue of gingerbread?

Why does the world before him
Melt in a million suns,
Why do his yellow, yearning eyes
Burn like saffron buns?

Watch where he comes walking
Out of the Christmas flame,
Dancing, double-talking:

Herod is his name.

At Nine of the Night I Opened
My Door

At nine of the night I opened my door
That stands midway between moor and moor,
And all around me, silver-bright,
I saw that the world had turned to white.

Thick was the snow on field and hedge
And vanished was the river-sedge,
Where winter skilfully had wound
A shining scarf without a sound.

And as I stood and gazed my fill
A stable-boy came down the hill.
With every step I saw him take
Flew at his heel a puff of flake.

His brow was whiter than the hoar,
A beard of freshest snow he wore,
And round about him, snowflake starred,
A red horse-blanket from the yard.

In a red cloak I saw him go,
His back was bent, his step was slow,
And as he laboured through the cold
He seemed a hundred winters old.

I stood and watched the snowy head,
The whiskers white, the cloak of red.
'A Merry Christmas!' I heard him cry.
'The same to you, old friend,' said I.

Singing Game

The Round House, *c.* 1830, is built over a broken
market cross at Newport, Launceston, in Cornwall.

Here we go round the Round House
In the month of one,
Looking to the eastward
For the springing sun.
The sky is made of ashes,
The trees are made of bone,
And all the water in the well
Is stubborn as a stone.

Here we go round the Round House
In the month of two,
Waiting for the weather
To thaw my dancing shoe.
In St Thomas River
Hide the freckled trout,
But for dinner on Friday
I shall pull one out.

Here we go round the Round House
In the month of three,
Listening for the bumble
Of the humble-bee.
The light is growing longer,
The geese begin to lay,
The song-thrush in the churchyard
Charms the cold away.

Here we go round the Round House
In the month of four,
Watching a couple dressed in green
Dancing through the door.
One wears a wreath of myrtle,
Another, buds of thorn:
God grant that all men's children
Be as sweetly born.

Here we go round the Round House
In the month of five,
Waiting for the summer
To tell us we're alive.
All round the country
The warm seas flow,
The devil's on an ice-cap
Melting with the snow.

Here we go round the Round House
In the month of six;
High in the tower
The town clock ticks.
Hear the black quarter-jacks
Beat the noon bell;
They say the day is half away
And the year as well.

Here we go round the Round House
In the month of seven,
The river running thirsty
From Cornwall to Devon.
The sun is on the hedgerow,
The cattle in the stream,

And one will give us strawberries
And one will give us cream.

Here we go round the Round House
In the month of eight,
Hoping that for harvest
We shall never wait.
Slyly the sunshine
Butters up the bread
To bear us through the winter
When the light is dead.

Here we go round the Round House
In the month of nine,
Watching the orchard apple
Turning into wine.
The day after tomorrow
I'll take one from the tree
And pray the worm will do no harm
If it comes close to me.

Here we go round the Round House
In the month of ten,
While the cattle winter
In the farmer's pen.
Thick the leaves are lying
On the coppice floor;
Such a coat against the cold
Never a body wore.

Here we go round the Round House
In the month of eleven,

The sea-birds swiftly flying
To the coast of heaven.
The plough is in the furrow,
The boat is on the strand;
May I be fed on fish and bread
While water lies on land.

Here we go round the Round House
In the month of twelve,
The hedgers break the brier
And the ditchers delve.
As we go round the Round House
May the moon and sun
Guide us to tomorrow
And the month of one:
And life be never done.

John Fuller

John Fuller was born in Ashford, Kent, in 1937. He was educated at St Paul's School and at New College, Oxford, where he was awarded the Newdigate Prize in 1960. He is the son of another poet, Roy Fuller. In 1962/3 he was Visiting Lecturer at the State University of New York, Buffalo, and from 1963 to 1966 Assistant Lecturer at Manchester University. Since 1966 he has been a Fellow of Magdalen College, Oxford. He lives in Oxford, with his wife and three daughters. His awards include the Richard Hillary Memorial Prize (1961) and the Faber Memorial Prize (1974); in 1983 his first work of adult fiction, *Flying to Nowhere*, won the Whitbread Memorial Prize and was shortlisted for the Booker Prize.

His published poetry includes *Fairground Music* (1961) and *The Tree That Walked* (1967), both published by Chatto & Windus: *Cannibals and Missionaries* (1972), *The Mountain in the Sea* (1975), *Lies and Secrets* (1979) and *The Beautiful Inventions* (1983), all published by Secker & Warburg. His two collections for children are *Squeaking Crust* (Chatto & Windus, 1974) and *Come Aboard and Sail Away* (Salamander, 1983). As a critic he has published books on eighteenth-century poetry, on the sonnet and on the writer W. H. Auden.

The poems in this collection are taken from *Allsorts* (a children's annual, Macmillan 1968–76), *The Beautiful Inventions*, *Come Aboard and Sail Away*, *Fairground Music*, *Herod Do Your Worst* (Novello, 1968), *Lies and Secrets*, *Over the Bridge* (Kestrel and Puffin, 1981), *Squeaking Crust* and *The Mountain in the Sea*.

Adam's Apple and *The Ship of Sounds* were written in collaboration with the composer Bryan Kelly. *Fox-Trot* and *Half a Fortnight* were also written with Bryan Kelly and were originally commissioned by the Leicestershire Schools Festival of Music.

Although John Fuller is a poet, he rates music as the greatest of the arts and wishes he himself were not such an inefficient pianist. Even so, he enjoys playing the piano with his daughters and his students; especially, at present, the works of Poulenc, Milhaud and Fauré.

I might have guessed at his love for music. Many of his poems are written in linked sequences with a composer friend, Bryan Kelly, and have been performed by school-children. The stimulus he gets from music influences his poetry. Sometimes you can hear the tune strongly as you read aloud or silently; in the 'Polka' poem from *Fox-Trot* for instance, the words dance along. At other times the lilt is gently suggested, subtler – as in 'Mary, Queen of Scots' Song'.

John Fuller's pleasure in rhythmic verse dates back to his schooldays, when poems such as Masefield's 'Sea Fever' and W. B. Yeats's 'The Fiddler of Dooney' were among those he would recite or copy into his personal anthology. This led, later, to the poetry of T. S. Eliot and Wallace Stevens, and W. H. Auden's early verse.

Traditional forms of poetry writing, like ballads and sonnets, have rules and boundaries, in much the same way as games do. You learn to respect and enjoy and to master the rules; and from the discipline of line-lengths, number of beats, and rhyme pattern you discover how to develop your own style further. John Fuller likens this to a similar discipline in painting: 'When a child I loved being taught things like perspective: I found them liberating. Sploshing around with finger paints is no good. There's no indication of what you are meant to do. No rules.'

This is an important theory when you look at the immense freedom and originality of John Fuller's writing;

his rich and often unexpected vocabulary; the play on words; the feeling that he has explored and relished his ideas to their limit.

I visited him at Magdalen College, Oxford, in a room filled with books and colour and warmth and a lively feeling of plenty going on. Books by and about W. H. Auden predominated: after I left, a student would arrive for a tutorial on this poet's work, a subject on which John Fuller is a noted authority. A game of chess was in progress on a low table: he plays mostly by correspondence, or with a computer. 'You can ration the time spent on thinking about the moves that way.'

Another interest is printing. He has an old press and sets up poems by hand and prints pamphlets, by a method that has changed little since the fifteenth century. He has even made his own paper, and finds that messing around with oily machinery can be very relaxing and a change from teaching.

The Fuller family live in Oxford but like to get away to their cottage on the Lleyn Peninsula as often as possible. The Welsh countryside has influenced John Fuller's writing, and at least three collections of poetry have been largely written there. Life in this beautiful country makes a contrast to his busy working life in Oxford, where besides teaching English and doing research he is involved in plenty of college administration.

'Sitting on a committee is very different from sitting 1,700 feet up on a cairn, but I don't suppose I'd like to do either without the other. That's perhaps something else to remember about poetry: contrast, drama and paradox are its essence.'

from *Fox-Trot*

AUBADE

As the earth's turning darkness ends,
Night and the landscape part like friends
    With tearful eyes.
The sun is leaning out of bed
Better to hear what's being said,
    Too snug to rise.

The morning's dews though fresh and sweet
Would strike his warm ensheeted feet
    As rather damp.
He'll wait an hour. It's much too soon
To more than stretch, until the moon
    Has doused her lamp.

Another day has lit each farm
Where cock-a-doodles boast that harm
    Has passed them by.
They strut into the coops and count
Their hens. If there's the right amount
    They crow and cry:

'O blessed dawn! O doodle-doo!
O daylight, how we longed for you!
    Our beaks we raise
And for our preservation through
A night of terrors welcome you
    In vocal praise.'

But here and there a dreadful quiet
Or lamentation, grief and riot
   Will greet your ear.
A hen is missing! Count again!
But scattered feathers, eight, nine, ten,
   Confirm his fear.

'Ah me! Unlucky me! Alas!
Now the worst has come to pass:
   My hen is stolen!'
Instead of welcoming the dawn
The cock is silent and forlorn.
   His crest is fallen.

The farmer comes and rubs his beard:
Who does by night what he's afeared
   To do by day?
The farmer knows, but it is time
The sun should rise to light the crime
   With searching ray.

Upon the earth still moist with dew
The farmer finds the bedded clue
   Of pad and claw,
And now he knows that he is right
For he has seen the dreaded sight
   Of fox's paw!

POLKA

A fox don't make a faux pas!
   Oh no, sir!
We have our family pride.
We're very very proper
And it makes us warm inside.
We like to see some action
And we're nifty on our paws.
There's a glow of satisfaction
With a bird between your jaws.
But we're very very proper.
We don't do it without cause.
We have to have our *breakfast*
(We have our family pride)
We *have* to have our breakfast
For it makes us warm inside.

A fox don't make a faux pas!
   Oh no, sir!
We're gentlemen through and through.
No grasping interloper,
It's 'please!' and 'after you!'
We like our small adventures,
We like to come and go:
A duck between your dentures?
Well done! Oh damn' good show!
No grasping interloper
We'd have you jolly well know.
Our tastes are very *civilized*
(We're gentlemen through and through)
Our *tastes* are very civilized
And it's 'please!' and 'after you!'

FUNERAL MARCH

Here come the hounds alive from the kennels,
Keen for their taste of Mr Reynolds.

Here comes the Master with set lips.
Here comes the Huntsman. Here come the Whips.

Here comes the Hunt in black and red,
Colour of death and colour of blood.

The Hunt is after you. Beware!
O Mr Reynolds, take care, take care!

A cup is raised in the village square.
A bell rings roundly through the air.

How quiet the meadows, like a sea
Shifting the wrecks of woods so silently!

The bell rings out and rings its fill
And all the little farms are still.

The Hunt is setting off. Beware!
O Mr Reynolds, take care, take care!

Past the church and through a gate
Trots in line the fox's fate.

The cautious Huntsman slows and stops.
The hounds are worrying a nearby copse.

O Mr Reynolds, were you there?
And left your odour on the air?

The eager hounds from nose to tail
Quiver as they sniff your trail.

They lift their ears, and growl and whine,
Then openly they own the line.

Hear the horn and holloas sing!
Hear the pack's wild yelping ring!

Hear the smallest rider's shout:
Oh they will surely find you out!

The hounds are busy and intent,
Now feathering to chase the scent.

Now the Huntsman's viewed his quarry.
Danger, Mr Reynolds, hurry!

There, there beyond the stream –
A brush of russet tipped with cream.

Now disappearing in the trees,
Padding softly at his ease.

The Hunt is after you. Beware!
O Mr Reynolds, take care, take care!

The hounds are breathing at my tail.
The Hunt behind is in full cry,
　　Grimly grim.
The Master knows he will not fail
To see his tiring quarry die,
　　Horrible him!

Another fence won't keep them back.
They have the panic scent too strong,
　　Grimly grim.
The Master close behind the pack
Knows that now he can't go wrong,
　　Horrible him!

Now I am running for my life.
The Hunt's upon me in a rush,
　　Grimly grim.
The Master holds a little knife
With which to amputate my brush,
　　Horrible him!

How to Open

SARDINES

You don't have to grope in a
Drawer for an opener:
Sardines have a key and a lock.
There's a horrible slit
That you fit on a lip,
And you turn like you're winding a clock.

It's blunt and it's bendable,
Thin and expendable,
Useless except for sardines.
You can easily lose it,
And just try to use it
On cylinder-shaped tins of beans.

It functions for feasting
Just once (like a bee-sting)
And doesn't grow rust in a drawer.
It curls up with the tin
Till it's stuck fast within,
And can't ever be used any more.

BEANS

The tin-opener is a handleable sort of rhinoceros,
Snub and bumbling, but sharp as a pair of binoculars.
It is by the kind use of his snout
That the beans come shlurping out.

[75]

Bilberries

I

Late in the season: reason then not to wait.

Frown as you climb: time to smile going down.

See the spring: ling lifts and is a bee.

Drop to your knees: pleased to be where you stop.

Blue under green: seen, and seen first, by you.

Linger on the scree: greed's purple finger.

Bilberry flan, bilberry flan:
Leave off eating where you began.

Bilberry tart, bilberry tart,
Large and sweet as a courtier's heart.

Bilberry jam, bilberry jam:
Sometimes we eat it with roast lamb.

Bilberry fool, bilberry fool:
Whip it with cream and let it cool.

Bilberry crumble, bilberry crumble:
Too-big mouthfuls make you mumble.

June to August we will pick
Bilberries until we're sick.

from *Half a Fortnight*

THURSDAY

Skipping to the shop on Thursday, ice-cream for you and
    me,
  I skipped right back on the pavement cracks
For Thursday is a half-day, its afternoon is free.
    Good as five new pennies,
    True as a chippy's eye,
    Followed my father to Leicester
    And made my mother cry,
    Stood my brother in a corner
    With his left shoe on his right,
    Didn't come back till half past nine
    And ate ice-cream all night.

Skipping to the shop on Thursday, for humbugs white
    and brown,
  Back I tripped and the long rope flippéd
For Thursday is a half-day and all its blinds were down.
    Good as a fresh-plucked cherry,
    True as a double twenty,
    Helped myself from the pudding shelf
    But left my father plenty,
    Stood my brother on a promise
    And skipped all night through Devon,
    Sharpened knives in old St Ives
    And didn't come back till seven.

Skipping to the shop on Thursday, for liquorice long and
    black,

There was no one to sell when I rang the bell
For Thursday is a half-day, and I skipped the whole way
    back.
    Good as an indian summer,
    True as a billiard cue,
    Used my sister's lipstick
    And made my eyelids blue,
    Stood my brother no longer,
    Left him on the wall,
    Skipped away and skipped all day
    And never came back at all.

FRIDAY

A dry wind on Friday hurries the leaves
Into drifts under walls and piles in odd places
And the yard is a brown storm of death and air.
One bird in a shabby coat looking at faces,
Dry-veined faces of leaves in the courtyard,
Sees in curled shapes the strength that was there
When laughing summer shook his long green hair
And the air was fresh and warm and full of birds.

A cold wind on Friday flattens the leaves
And freezes their veins and darkens their colour
And the yard is a still grave of leaves and frost.
One bird in a ruffled coat seeing the pallor,
Snow-burdened pallor of sky through the bare trees,
Sees in veined shapes the warmth that was lost
When golden autumn hugged to death and tossed
His precious fruit and leaves and birds away.

A wet wind on Friday loses the leaves
Which sink to the soil when the winter comes
And the yard is a white square of ice and snow.
One bird in a tattered coat looking for crumbs,
Half-hidden crumbs in the cold empty courtyard,
Sees in those shapes the love that you owe
When iron winter sinks and will not go
And all the leaves and all the birds are gone.

SUNDAY

Tip-top, stirrup-strap, tip-top, stirrup-strap,
Tip-top, stirrup-strap, straw!
Trotting on the gravel by the old canal
With a flat black barge to draw,
The mist's still on the meadow
And the Sunday sleepers snore.

The birds sing loud for Charlie,
The skylark and the linnet,
The swans make way for Charlie
(Tchaikovsky isn't in it)
And sparrows on his panama
Sit talking by the minute.

Chup-twee, ticker-ticker, chup-twee, ticker-ticker,
Chup-twee, ticker-ticker, ting!
Trotting on the gravel by tasty hedges
Where the sparrows sing
Like choristers in churches
Where the Sunday bellmen ring.

What does a barge-horse think of
As he makes the towpath bend?
Does he think the harness worth it
To be the birds' best friend?
And does he dream of scratching-posts
At half a fortnight's end?

Scratch-scratch, wiggle-wiggle, scratch-scratch, wiggle-
        wiggle,
Scratch-scratch, wiggle-wiggle, scratch!
Trotting on the gravel with an old red blanket
And a panama hat to match,
With flannels flashing on the green
Where the Sunday fielders catch.

Charlie, O Charlie
You've earned a holiday,
And all the Sunday children
Will run to you to play,
And bring you lumps of sugar
And wisps of summer hay.

So tip-top, stirrup-strap, tip-top, stirrup-strap,
Tip-top, stirrup-strap, straw!
Trotting on the gravel as day is ending
And Sunday curtains draw,
When the mist creeps up on the meadow
And the Sunday sleepers snore.

Topkapi

I am the sultan. Jewelled, I sit on jewels.
My head bows with the weight of jewels.
My fingers curl open with the weight of jewels.

They bring me a bowl of emeralds the size of figs
To play with if I want to, and curds
To eat with spoons so diamonded
They rasp my lower lip.

I have a candlestick
With 6666 diamonds. The British Queen
Has sent me the jewelled order of her garter.

One day I will throw myself into the Bosphorus.

from *Songs for a Condemned Queen*

MARY QUEEN OF SCOTS' SONG

I wove this thread,
Gold, blue and red,
A thousand times till fingers bled.
   But it was all for show
   And I am weary now.

A thousand times,
A thousand times,
The stitches met like little rhymes.
   But it was all for show
   And I am weary now.

Bull, fish and lark
And half the Ark
And pretty dogs that try to bark.
   But it was all for show
   And I am weary now.

The fowls and apes
Are simply shapes:
The frozen fancy glares and gapes.
   For it was all for show
   And I am weary now.

The silver moth
Is still and wroth
To suffer in the prisoned cloth.

For it was all for show
And I am weary now.

The needle's art
Has played its part
To animate my heavy heart.
    But it was all for show
    And I am weary now.

The water roars
On death's dark shores
And what I thought was mine is yours.
    For it was all for show
    And I am weary now.

THE STABLE BOY'S SONG

    I sleep in straw
    That buzzes in my ears,
    I sleep in straw
    That tickles my nose,
    I sleep in straw
    With straw in my mouth
And dream of the great grey horses that pull the hay.

Laddie, laddie, light the lamps, laddie,
Link-light, laddie, light the lamps.
    One for a little boy,
    One for a queen,
And one for the grey goose on the may green.

I wake at five
With a hand on my shoulder,
I wake at five
With cramp in my bones,
I wake at five
And the world is dead
For night has his cold black hands on the earth's eyes still.

Laddie, laddie, light the lamps, laddie,
Link-light, laddie, light the lamps.
    One for a little boy,
    One for a queen,
And one for the grey goose on the may green.

    I light my torch
    With a flint's secrets,
    I light my torch
    At the sign of dusk,
    I light my torch
    To protect the castle
And brighten the twelve true lamps on the castle walls.

Laddie, laddie, light the lamps, laddie,
Link-light, laddie, light the lamps.
    One for a little boy,
    One for a queen,
And one for the grey goose on the may green.

Alex at the Barber's

He is having his hair cut. Towels are tucked
About his chin, his mop scalped jokingly.
The face in the mirror is his own face.

The barber moves and chats among the green
And methylated violet, snipper-snips,
Puts scissors down, plugs in a plaited flex,

And like a surgeon with his perfumed hands
Presses the waiting skull and shapes the base.
He likes having his hair cut, and the man

Likes cutting it. The radio drones on.
The eyes in the mirror are his own eyes.
While the next chair receives the Demon Blade,

A dog-leg razor nicks a sideburn here;
As from a sofa there a sheet is whisked
And silver pocketed. The doorbell pings.

The barber, frowning, grips the ragged fringe
And slowly cuts. Upon the speckled sheet
The bits fall down and now his hair is cut.

The neighing trams outside splash through the rain.
The barber tests the spray for heat and rubs
Lemon shampoo into his spiky hair.

Bent with his head above the running bowl,
Eyes squeezed shut, he does not see the water
Gurgle and sway like twisted sweetpaper

Above the waste, but, for a moment, tows
A sleigh of polished silver parrots through
Acres of snow, exclaiming soundlessly.

Then towel round head. Head swung gently up.
Eyes padded. As the barber briskly rubs,
The smile in the mirror is his own smile.

Sheep Party

Under thorn and bramble
The sheep have left their rags
And decorate the valley
With little woollen flags.

'This way to the party,'
The wispy tufts declare,
'Between the banks and hedges,
Hurry, you're nearly there!

'There's bracken newly curling
And bilberry in bloom,
The guests are quite contented
And there's lots and lots of room.'

But who am I to follow
And which way should I go?
The wool is blue and crimson
And from different sheep, I know.

The red-stained sheep live *that* way,
The blue-stained sheep up *there*.
There must be several parties
And I really couldn't care.

For I like peanut butter
Not grass and twigs and stones
Like the red sheep of Mr Roberts
And the blue of Mr Jones.

Creatures

The butterfly, alive inside a box,
Beats with its powdered wings in soundless knocks
And wishes polythene were hollyhocks.

The beetle clambering across the road
Appears to find his body quite a load:
My fingers meddle with his highway code

And slugs are rescued from the fatal hiss
Of tyres that kiss like zigzagged liquorice
On zigzagged liquorice, but sometimes miss.

Two snails are raced across a glistening stone
(Each eye thrust forward like a microphone)
So slowly that the winner is unknown.

To all these little creatures I collect
I mean no cruelty or disrespect
Although their day-by-day routine is wrecked.

They may remember their experience,
Though at the time it made no sort of sense,
And treat it with a kind of reverence.

It may be something that they never mention,
An episode outside their apprehension
Like some predestined intervention.

The Cricket

The cricket, like a knuckled rubber-band,
Whirrs from the launching platform of my hand
Without much notion where he's going to land.

But does he mind the jump or the surprise?
Suppose we chanced to be each other's size?
I know I wouldn't stay. I'd shut my eyes

And jump. Are bodies chosen with a pin?
My own seems suitable for being in,
But why pale pink, rather than pale green skin?

And does some giant, wishing me no harm,
Peruse me, perfect, on his unseen palm?
What creatures stir upon the cricket's arm?

The worlds are gears upon the wheels of chance.
The worlds retreat and worlds in worlds advance.
The creatures dance. And lead themselves a dance.

Leaping the grasses like a leafy lancer,
The cricket does not know that he's a dancer.
I ask the questions but he *is* the answer

And all the summer's day he needn't think
But simply jump, a jointed tiddlywink,
A perfect alpha minus in green ink.

from *Adam's Apple*

A WHOLE NEW SCENE

God leaned out of himself one day,
Said Hey out there, now what do you say?
I want to do something, I don't know what,
But whatever it is, I want it a lot.
He looked around, said Well, I declare!
There's absolutely nothing there!
He scratched his head and rubbed his chin:
What a predicament I'm in!
   I've got to
   Make a
Six-day war on chaos,
Six-day war on the Primitive Soup. I've got
Just six days in which to do it,
Six of the best for the empty vacuum,
A week of wonder for a whole new scene.

So God created the firmament
But God only knows what he thought he meant:
He put angels here and angels there
With nothing to do and no one to care.
He looked around, said Bless my soul!
That Satan thinks he's top of the poll.
Can't have him prying into my affairs.
I'll clip his wings and kick him downstairs.
   I've got to
   Make a
Six-day war on pride,

Six-day war on disobedience. I've got
Just six days in which to do it,
Six of the best for the Prince of Darkness,
A week of wonder for a whole new scene.

Then God got back to work and soon
He'd earth and trees and sun and moon.
What an invention! What an invention!
Come along to the World Convention!
Flowers burst open, fishes swim
And little birds fly up to him.
He's put those atoms through their paces
And now they're wearing their birthday faces
   Because he's
   Made a
Six-day war on chaos,
Six-day war on the Great Big Nothing. He had
Just six days in which to do it,
Six of the best (and by God he did it),
A week of wonder for a whole new scene.

PUTTING A NAME TO IT

All creation's got to have a name
Whether it's scaly, feathered, smooth or hairy.
If you don't know what it is, why that's a shame,
   And if you think the words won't fit,
   Well, definition
   Is Adam's mission:
It's a great big glorious game.
   Not Come here, that there!
   Or Hey, thingummy-bob!

Since Adam's been around:
Now we've got kangaroos and wallabies
And chimpanzees with alibis
And nightingales for lullabies
And slugs to give you willoughbies,
We've gallopers and lollopers
And crawlers on the syllabus
    Since all creation's got to have a name.

Yes, all creation's got to have a name,
So here's a man who's a walking dictionary
And every word is an animal's personal fame.
    One time it looked as if he'd quit
    But when it came to it
    He put a name to it:
It's a great big glorious game.
    Not Come on, you!
    Or Hey, what-do-you-call-it!
    Since Adam's been around
Now we've got okapis and antelopes
And wombats eating cantaloupes
And gibbons doing loop-the-loops
And hedgehogs rolling into hoops
And penguins forming into groups
Or falling in the water (oops!)
    Since all creation's got to have a name.

FORBIDDEN FRUIT

Adam and Eve, Adam and Eve,
Now don't you eat that apple or you'll make me grieve.
There's every kind of thrill for a vegetarian,

An innocent diet for a pre-lapsarian
Adam and Eve, Adam and Eve,
Now don't you eat that apple or you'll make me grieve.

> There's melons in the grass
> Growing so big,
> Get stoned on cherries
> And I don't care a fig,
> You can eat those grapes
> Till your mouth runs red
> And let the vine-leaves
> Go to your head,
> But the Tree of the Knowledge
> Of Good and of Evil
> Is forbidden to you
> Or you go to the Devil.

Adam and Eve, Adam and Eve,
Now don't you eat that apple or you'll make me grieve,
Adam and Eve.

ADAM'S APPLE

We told you it would happen.
It's written in the book.
But even though we knew it
We hardly dare to look.
                    Adam's apple.

Her mouth closed on the surface
And left a little bite
Just as Satan had advised
Although it didn't seem right.
        Adam's apple.

She gave the fruit to Adam
Who took a few bites more.
They liked that rosy apple
And wolfed it to the core.
        Adam's apple.

Then they knew they were guilty.
Then they knew about sin,
Looked at each other's bodies
Covered in nothing but skin.
        Adam's apple.

We didn't know we were naked.
We didn't know we were weak.
We thought we would last forever
But now the future's bleak.
        Adam's apple.

There once was a man with his head full of words
For animals, flowers and fishes and birds.
He lived in a garden with nothing to do
But keep it a-growing and keep himself true.
    Oh Adam, you silly man,
      You were riding for a fall:
      One little apple and you ruined us all.

He wanted a woman, he wanted a friend:
That old temptation, where will it end?
Eve ate the apple and Adam did too.
Together they bit their world in two.
    Oh Adam, you silly man,
      You were riding for a fall:
      One little apple and you ruined us all.

There's a lock-out in Eden, the pickets are there,
A beautiful angel with flaming hair.
He opened the gates and he pushed them through
And now they are mortal like me and you.
    Oh Adam, you silly man,
      You were riding for a fall:
      One little apple and you ruined us all.

Yes, one little apple without permission
Accounts for the whole of the human condition.
East of Eden the family grew
Raising Cain and feeling blue.
    Oh Adam, you silly man,
      You were riding for a fall:
      One little apple and you ruined us all.

from *The Ship of Sounds*

WHAT DOES THE WIND SAY?

What does the wind say
As the birdlike topsail shifts?
'Come aboard and sail away!'
And the ship of music drifts
And the warm air hums in the cross-trees
Beneath a burning sky
And the Bosun dreams of duck and peas
Of parasols and swarming bees
That vanish with a sigh.

What does the wind say
As the rigging creaks and strains?
'Come aboard and sail away
Down the salty ocean lanes!'
And the stopped air pipes in the cross-trees,
The sun's bright as a sword
And the Bosun whistles: '*If* you please!'
(And every one of the crew agrees)
As the Captain steps aboard.

What does the wind say
As the bellied mainsail swells?
'Come aboard and sail away!
The air is full of bells!'
And the sailors lean from the cross-trees,
Hanging by their socks,
To see the Bosun bend his knees,
To see the Bosun dance and squeeze
His little pleated box.

The skies fall in and the ocean raves,
Rhythm's the only thing we know,
Only the rhythm makes us row
And the sun is black and our heads are low:
    Whisper of voices, clink of chains,
    Clink of voices, whisper of chains,
    Whisper of voices that made us slaves
      So long ago.

Stroke of the cat and slap of the waves,
Rhythm's the only thing we know,
Only the rhythm makes us row
And the sun is black and our heads are low:
    Patter of drum and crack of whip,
    Crack of drum and patter of whip,
    Patter of drum and lashes for knaves
      Who pull too slow.

Sliding in fear over bottomless caves,
Rhythm's the only thing we know,
Only the rhythm makes us row
And the sun is black and our heads are low:
    Wrists together, reach and pull,
    Twist and feather, the blades are full,
    Pulling together over our graves
      Wherever we go.

Lulled by the heat
The ship's a cradle
So dry that we forget
The loves we left
In long harbour,
That sang in dreams
And sweetened labour,
So dry that nets are salt
And toes are leather,
So dry that we forget
The song we heard
On distant quays
That caught in sails
And brought us ease,
So dry, so dry
And deaf with heat
On the straw decks
When there are songs enough
In the green fields,
Lilies for pulling,
Inviting to leap
In the singing fields,
The fields of the sea,
The glittering green
Of the cool deep
Musical sea.

THE SHIP OF SOUNDS

Now let us have a catch, sir!
And stir our sluggish stumps, sir!
We'll batten down the hatch, sir!
And tread the deck with thumps, sir,
And tread the deck with thumps.

The best thing for the dumps, sir!
Is swigging back a drop, sir!
Then lacing on our pumps, sir!
To foot a skip and hop, sir,
To foot a skip and hop.

Your partner is a mop, sir!
With very bony knees, sir!
Don't hold her by the top, sir!
For goodness sake don't squeeze, sir,
For goodness sake don't squeeze.

Now everyone agrees, sir!
A way to keep awake, sir!
Is dancing on the seas, sir!
Like Nelson and like Drake, sir,
Like Nelson and like Drake.

It's music that we make, sir!
Our dancing knows no bounds, sir!
Whatever course we take, sir!
Upon the ship of sounds, sir,
Upon the ship of sounds.

Geography Lesson

With Highland hair and arms of Wales
Reaching for Ireland, England trails
A lonely distance behind Europe
Trying impossibly to cheer up:
A sloppy nurse who hopes that maybe
No one will see she's dropped her baby
Splash into the Irish Sea
While bouncing it upon her knee.

With hips of Norfolk, bum of Kent,
Her posture's more than strangely bent.
Yorkshire gives backache with its Ridings.
The Midlands, full of railway sidings,
She blames for burps of indigestion.
Her Birmingham has got congestion.
Her Derbyshire is full of holes.
London's asleep at the controls
And her subconscious shifts the worry
Out to Middlesex and Surrey.

Yet Devon's a comfortable shoe
From which old Cornwall's toes peep through.
On Lleyn, sedately, Anglesey
Is balanced like a cup of tea,
While clucking in her tea-time mirth
Her mouth's the open Solway Firth
Ready to swallow if she can
The little cake of the Isle of Man.

Even asleep she falls apart:
Dreams of the Orkneys make her start
And stitches of the Isle of Wight
Drop off from Hampshire in the night.
With bits of knitting in the Channel,
Most of East Anglia wrapped in flannel
And snores exhaling from Argyll,
The dear old lady makes you smile:
What can you do with such a creature
To whom each county lends a feature?
She'll still be there when I am gone.
Through all *your* lives she'll shamble on,
Grubby, forgetful, laughing, hatless –
The silliest country in the atlas.

Lullaby

Sleep little baby, clean as a nut,
Your fingers uncurl and your eyes are shut.
Your life was ours, which is with you.
Go on your journey. We go too.

The bat is flying round the house
Like an umbrella turned into a mouse.
The moon is astonished and so are the sheep:
Their bells have come to send you to sleep.

Oh be our rest, our hopeful start.
Turn your head to my beating heart.
Sleep little baby, clean as a nut,
Your fingers uncurl and your eyes are shut.

Tides

It's time to go, but still we sit
Lingering in our summer
Like idle fingers,
Like fingers in the sand.

Or like a tiny snail that moves
Beneath a gravelly pool,
Taking its life to travel,
Taking between the tides.

Elizabeth Jennings

Elizabeth Jennings was born in Boston, Lincolnshire, in July 1926, and educated at Oxford High School and St Anne's College, Oxford.

She worked at Oxford City Library, and then as a reader for Chatto & Windus. Since 1961 she has been a freelance writer and critic. She received an Arts Council Award in 1953, the Somerset Maugham Award in 1956, and the Richard Hillary Memorial Prize in 1966. She lives in Oxford.

Her publications include *A Way of Looking* (1955), *A Sense of the World* (1958), *Song for a Birth and a Death* (1961) and *Recoveries* (1964), all published by André Deutsch; *Collected Poems* (1967), *The Secret Brother* (1966) and *The Animals' Arrival* (1969), all published by Macmillan; *Growing Points* (Carcanet, 1975) and *After the Ark* (Oxford University Press, 1978). She has edited *Let's Have Some Poetry* (Museum Press, 1960) and *Anthology of Modern Verse* (Methuen, 1961).

The poems in this selection are taken from *After the Ark, The Animals' Arrival, Collected Poems, Growing Points* and *The Secret Brother*.

When I looked at some of my old school magazines recently I was embarrassed to read my early efforts at poetry: sentimental stuff on war, death and love, none of which I knew anything about. So I knew exactly how Elizabeth Jennings felt when she looked back at *her* first poetic attempts. They were ambitious, on subjects outside her own experience at the time. She wrote of hero-worship, patriotism and death. One of her favourite walks as a schoolgirl was round and round a graveyard, with a friend. Her mother thought this was very morbid behaviour but, in fact, the walk wasn't entirely gloomy; the two girls enjoyed laughing at the epitaphs on some of the graves.

She was thirteen when she first began to write, and was, she says, very young for her age. Her early poems were strict in metre and rhyme; she wrote sonnets, odes and ballads. Her interest in poetry was encouraged by excellent teaching at school, and she knows how lucky she was to have teachers who approached the subject both 'sensitively and sensibly'. The first poem she herself really loved and was moved by was G. K. Chesterton's splendid battle narrative, 'Lepanto'. When she told me this, lines like

From evening isles fantastical rings faint the Spanish gun,
And the Lord upon the Golden Horn is laughing in the
    sun...

sprang into my mind as vividly as when I was first roused by them. Not long after that the Romantic poets – Keats, Shelley, Wordsworth, Coleridge – caught her imagination; and later Browning.

Elizabeth Jennings is convinced that no poet can write poems of any real value without being steeped in the great traditions of verse, from Chaucer, through to Shakespeare, to present-day poets. She herself still reads copiously and often reviews current volumes of verse.

She took seriously T. S. Eliot's remark that 'a young poet hasn't anything to say', and that what was important was 'craftsmanship not content', and considers that her long apprenticeship with the tools of poetry gave her the means to write when she eventually found something worth writing about.

Her first interesting subject matter was the discovery of Italy, and of Florence in particular: then came Rome, where she spent two three-month periods in 1957 and 1958. She 'learnt' Rome as one learns a person one loves, and this meant of course trying to speak Italian. When she was older she wrote of her faith – she is a Catholic – and of her religious experience.

Next to literature, she would place painting as her second favourite art, and she loves looking at pictures. She is also an enthusiastic theatregoer. Her collection of what she calls 'little things' must be unique: her room is a store for small dolls, ornaments, dolls' house furniture and animals, tiny and brightly coloured and jostling for space, made of wood, glass and metal ... no plastic, she insists!

I've been an admirer of Elizabeth Jennings's work for a long time, and particularly of those poems that deal with love, friendships and family relationships. She has the ability gently to understate those sad bleak moments as well as the happy ones, and it is just that understatement that says so much. You learn to read between, and beneath, the lines. Through reading her poetry I've been persuaded to look with a fresh eye at myself, so it came as no surprise when she said, 'Writing poetry seemed to me to be another way of finding out what life and the world meant.'

Rhyme for Children

I am the seed that slept last night;
This morning I have grown upright.

Within my dream there was a king.
Now he is gone in the wide morning.

He had a queen, also a throne.
Waking, I find myself alone.

If I could have that dream again,
The seed should grow into a queen

And she should find at her right hand
A king to rule her heart and land:

And I would be the spring which burst
Beside their love and quenched their thirst.

The Secret Brother

Jack lived in the green-house
When I was six,
With glass and with tomato plants,
Not with slates and bricks.

I didn't have a brother,
Jack became mine.
Nobody could see him,
He never gave a sign.

Just beyond the rockery,
By the apple-tree,
Jack and his old mother lived,
Only for me.

With a tin telephone
Held beneath the sheet,
I would talk to Jack each night.
We would never meet.

Once my sister caught me,
Said, 'He isn't there.
Down among the flower-pots
Cramm the gardener

Is the only person.'
I said nothing, but
Let her go on talking.
Yet I moved Jack out.

He and his old mother
Did a midnight flit.
No one knew his number:
I had altered it.

Only I could see
The sagging washing-line
And my brother making
Our own secret sign.

Friends

I fear it's very wrong of me,
And yet I must admit,
When someone offers friendship
I want the *whole* of it.
I don't want everybody else
To share my friends with me.
At least, I want *one* special one,
Who, indisputably,

Likes me much more than all the rest,
Who's always on my side,
Who never cares what others say,
Who lets me come and hide
Within his shadow, in his house –
It doesn't matter where –
Who lets me simply be myself,
Who's always, *always* there.

Comfort

Hand closed upon another, warm.
The other, cold, turned round and met
And found a weather made of calm.
So sadness goes, and so regret.

A touch, a magic in the hand.
Not what the fortune-teller sees
Or thinks that she can understand.
This warm hand binds but also frees.

Holidays at Home

There was a family who, every year,
Would go abroad, sometimes to Italy,
Sometimes to France. The youngest did not dare
To say, 'I much prefer to stay right here.'

You see, abroad there were no slot-machines,
No bright pink rock with one name going through it,
No rain, no boarding-houses, no baked beans,
No landladies, and no familiar scenes.

And George, the youngest boy, so longed to say,
'I don't *like* Greece, I don't like all these views,
I don't like having fierce sun every day,
And, most of all, I just detest the way

The food is cooked – that garlic and that soup,
Those strings of pasta, and no cakes at all.'
The family wondered why George seemed to droop
And looked just like a thin hen in a coop.

They never guessed why when they said, 'Next year
We can't afford abroad, we'll stay right here',
George looked so pleased and soon began to dream
Of piers, pink rock, deep sand, and Devonshire cream.

Afterthought

For weeks before it comes I feel excited, yet when it
At last arrives, things all go wrong:
My thoughts don't seem to fit.
I've planned what I'll give everyone and what they'll give
     to me,
And then on Christmas morning all
The presents seem to be

Useless and tarnished. I have dreamt that everything
     would come
To life – presents and people too.
Instead of that, I'm dumb,

And people say, 'How horrid! What a sulky little boy!'
And they are right. I *can't* seem pleased.
The lovely shining toy

I wanted so much when I saw it in a magazine
Seems pointless now. And Christmas too
No longer seems to mean

The hush, the star, the baby, people being kind again.
The bells are rung, sledges are drawn,
And peace on earth for men.

Chop-suey

There was a man who in the East
Made sweet-sour soups, a Chinese feast
Of birds' nests, sharks' fins, pancake rolls,
And piles of rice with shrimps in bowls.

In many cities in the West
This man built cafés. Every guest
Was given plastic chopsticks and
A finger-bowl to wash each hand.

The menu written out was good
And many people liked the food.
The dishes offered pleased the young,
And *no one* jested, 'Who flung dung?'

Now every town and every street
Serves pancake rolls, pork sour and sweet,
And yet amongst the bamboo-shoots
We taste old hot-pots, chips, and sprouts.

Old People

Why are people impatient when they are old?
Is it because they are tired of trying to make
Fast things move slowly?
I have seen their eyes flinch as they watch the lorries
Lurching and hurrying past.
I have also seen them twitch and move away
When a grandbaby cries.
They can go to the cinema cheaply,
They can do what they like all day.
Yet they shrink and shiver, looking like old, used dolls.
I do not think that I should like to be old.

Tiffany: a Burmese Kitten

(who is real)

FOR MRS GRAHAM GREENE

My friends keep mice – white ones and patched.
I wish I could pretend
I really like the creatures, but
I cannot and I spend

Just hours and hours admiring them.
I think my friends soon guess
They're not my kind of animal.
My secret wish, oh, yes,

Is for a Burmese kitten, one
Of those pure chocolate brown
Cats that I know are seldom seen
In any usual town.

I once met one called Tiffany;
She used to come and see
Me when I was in hospital.
She'd jump all over me,

Knock flowers down, explore the place
From door to door, and leap
Up all the tawdry furniture.
I know she helped me sleep:

I know she helped me get quite well,
Although I did not see
That at the time she came she was
Doctor and nurse to me.

My Animals

My animals are made of wool and glass,
Also of wood. Table and mantelpiece
Are thickly covered with them. It's because
You cannot keep real cats or dogs in these

High-up new flats. I really want to have
A huge, soft marmalade or, if not that,
Some animal that *seems* at least to love.
Hamsters? A dog? No, what I need's a cat.

I hate a word like 'pets'; it sounds so much
Like something with no living of its own.
And yet each time that I caress and touch
My wool or glass ones, I feel quite alone.

No kittens in our flat, no dog to bark
Each time the bell rings. Everything is still;
Often I want a zoo, a whole Noah's ark.
Nothing is born here, nothing tries to kill.

The Animals' Arrival

So they came
Grubbing, rooting, barking, sniffing,
Feeling for cold stars, for stone, for some hiding-place,
Loosed at last from heredity, able to eat
From any tree or from ground, merely mildly themselves,
And every movement was quick, was purposeful, was
     proposed.
The galaxies gazed on, drawing in their distances.
The beasts breathed out warm on the air.

No-one had come to make anything of this,
To move it, name it, shape it a symbol;
The huge creatures were their own depth, the hills
Lived lofty there, wanting no climber.
Murmur of birds came, rumble of underground beasts
And the otter swam deftly over the broad river.

There was silence too.
Plants grew in it, it wove itself, it spread, it enveloped
The evening as day-calls died and the universe hushed,
     hushed.
A last bird flew, a first beast swam
And prey on prey
Released each other
(Nobody hunted at all):
They slept for the waiting day.

The Earthworm's Monologue

Birds prey on me, fish are fond of my flesh.
My body is like a sausage, it lacks the snake's
Sinuous splendour and colour. Yes, I'm absurd.
Yet I also till and soften the soil, I prepare
The way for flowers. Spring depends upon me
At least a little. Mock me if you will,
Cut me in half, I'll come together again.
But haven't you felt a fool, hated your shape,
Wanted to hide? If so I am your friend;
I would sympathize with you were I not so busy
But bend down over me, you who are not yet tall
And be proud of all you contain in a body so small.

The Moth's Plea

I am a disappointment
And much worse.
You hear a flutter, you expect a brilliance of wings,
Colours dancing, a bright
Flutter, but then you see
A brown, bedraggled creature
With a shamefaced, unclean look
Darting upon your curtains and clothes,
Fighting against the light.
I hate myself. It's no wonder you hate me.

I meddle among your things,
I make a meal out of almost any cloth,
I hide in cupboards and scare
Any who catch me unaware.
I am your enemy – the moth.

You try to keep me away
But I'm wily and when I do
Manage to hide, you chase me, beat me, put
Horrible-smelling balls to poison me.
Have you ever thought what it's like to be
A parasite,
Someone who gives you a fright,
Who envies the rainbow colours of the bright
Butterflies who hover round flowers all day?
O please believe that I do understand how it feels
To be awake in and be afraid of the night.

Wasp in a Room

Chase me, follow me round the room, knock over
Chairs and tables, bruise knees, spill books. High
I am then. If you climb up to me I go
Down. I have ways of detecting your least
Movements. I have radar you did not
Invent. You are afraid of me. I can
Sting hard. Ah but watch me bask in
The, to you, unbearable sun. I sport with it, am
Its jester and also its herald. Fetch a
Fly whisk. I scorn such. You must invent stings
For yourselves or else leave me alone, small, flying,
Buzzing tiger who have made a jungle out of the room you
       thought safe,
Secure from all hurts and prying.

The Ladybird's Story

It was a roadway to me.
So many meeting-places and directions.
It was smooth, polished, sometimes it shook a little
But I did not tumble off.
I heard you say, and it was like a siren,
'A ladybird. Good luck. Perhaps some money.'
I did not understand.
Suddenly I was frightened, fearful of falling
Because you lifted your hand.

And then I saw your eyes,
Glassy moons always changing shape,
Sometimes suns in eclipse.
I watched the beak, the peak of your huge nose
And the island of your lips.
I was afraid but you were not. I have
No sting. I do not wound.
I carry a brittle coat. It does not protect.
I thought you would blow me away but superstition
Saved me. You held your hand now in one position,
Gentled me over the veins and arteries.
But it was not I you cared about but money.
You see I have watched you with flies.

The Owl's Request

Do not be frightened of me.
I am a night-time creature. When the earth is still,
When trees are shadows of shadows,
When only the moon and its attendant stars
Enlarge the night, when the smallest sound is shrill
And may wake you up and frighten you,
I am about with my friendly 'Tu-whit, tu whoo'.

My face is kindly but also mysterious.
People call me wise.
Perhaps they do so because I sometimes close my eyes
And seem to be thinking.
The way I think is not like yours. I need
No thick philosopher's book;
I can tell the truth of the world with a look
But I do not speak about
What I see there. Think of me then
As the certainty in your wandering nights.
I can soothe men
And will snatch you out of your doubt,
Bear you away to the stars and moon
And to sleep and dawn. So lie
And listen to my lullaby.

The Sparrows' Chorus

How often you forget about us! We are
About all through the year.
Our feathers are drab, beside other birds we appear
Nonentities, no fashion parades for us.
Nobody makes a fuss
Of us and really we don't care,
At least, not too much.
But we are faithful, whatever the weather we stay
Among you. And don't think we're ungrateful for the food
Some of you like to toss.
We need it badly. We can lose half our weight
On an icy night. We depend a lot on you.

Often, we have to admit, we wish we wore
Flamboyant colours. A yellow, a red, a blue.
The robin is lucky and all the tits are too.
But perhaps our smallness is noticeable. Beside
A starling or blackbird we are almost invisible
But don't forget we are here,
Domestic creatures, never flying far.
Just to exist through an English climate is
Remarkable.
It's almost a miracle simply that we are.

The Fieldmouse's Monologue

Didn't you know how frightened I was when I came
For shelter in your room? I am not tame.
You looked enormous when I saw you first.
I rushed to the hole I had made, took refuge there,
Crouched behind paper you thrust at me, shivered with
    fear.
I had smelt some chocolate. The kitchen was warm below
And outside there was frost and, one whole night, great
    snow.

I only guessed you were frightened too when you
Called out loudly, deafeningly to me.
My ears are small but my hearing strong, you see.
You pushed old papers against my hole and so
I had to climb into a drawer. You did not know
That I could run so high. I felt your hand,
Like my world in shadow, shudder across me and
I scuttled away but felt a kind of bond
With you in your huge fear.
Was I the only friend near?

The Rabbit's Advice

I have been away too long.
Some of you think I am only a nursery tale,
One which you've grown out of.
Or perhaps you saw a movie and laughed at my ears
But rather envied my carrot.
I must tell you that I exist.

I'm a puff of wool leaping across a field,
Quick to all noises,
Smelling my burrow of safety.
I am easily frightened. A bird
Is tame compared to me.
Perhaps you have seen my fat white cousin who sits,
Constantly twitching his nose,
Behind bars in a hutch at the end of a garden.
If not, imagine those nights when you lie awake
Afraid to turn over, afraid
Of night and dawn and sleep.
Terror is what I am made
Of partly, partly of speed.

But I am a figure of fun.
I have no dignity
Which means I am never free.
So, when you are frightened or being teased, think of
My twitching whiskers, my absurd white puff of a tail,
Of all that I mean by 'me'
And my ludicrous craving for love.

The Hedgehog's Explanation

I move very slowly,
I would like to be friendly,
Yet my prickly back has a look of danger. You might
Suppose I were ready for war or at least a fight
With a cat on the wall, a gather of birds, but no,
My prickles damage nobody, so you

Must be gentle with me, you with your huge shadow,
Your footsteps like claps of thunder,
The terrible touch of your hands.
Listen to me: I am a ball of fear,
Terror is what I know best,
What I live with and dream about.
Put out a saucer of milk for me,
Keep me from roads and cars.
If *you* want to look after someone,
Take care of me
And give me at least the pretence I am safe and free.

The Sheep's Confession

I look stupid, much like a dirty heap of snow
The Winter left.
I have nothing to draw your attention, nothing for show,
Except the craft

Which shears me and leaves me looking even more
Unintelligent.
I do not wonder you laugh when you see my bare
Flesh like a tent

Whose guy-ropes broke. But listen, I have one thing
To charm and delight –
The lamb I drop when Winter is turning to Spring.
His coat is white,

Purer than mine and he wears socks of black wool.
He can move
And prance. I am proud of a son so beautiful
And so worthy of love.

The Deers' Request

We are the disappearers.
You may never see us, never,
But if you make your way through a forest
Stepping lightly and gently,
Not plucking or touching or hurting,
You may one day see a shadow
And after the shadow a patch
Of speckled fawn, a glint
Of a horn.
    Those signs mean us.

O chase us never. Don't hurt us.
We who are male carry antlers
Horny, tough, like trees,
But we are terrified creatures,
Are quick to move, are nervous
Of the flutter of birds, of the quietest
Footfall, are frightened of every noise.

If you would learn to be gentle,
To be quiet and happy alone,
Think of our lives in deep forests,
Of those who hunt us and haunt us
And drive us into the ocean.
If you love to play by yourself
Content in that liberty,
Think of us being hunted,
Tell those men to let us be.

The Animals' Chorus

Once there was nothing but water and air. The air
Broke into constellations, waters withdrew.
The sun was born and itself hatched out first light.
Rocks appeared and sand, and on the rocks
There was movement. Under the sea
Something tender survived, not yet a fish,
A nameless object floating. This was how we

Began and how you later followed us,
Much, much later, long before clocks or sun-dials,
Long before time was discovered.
The sun stared hard and the moon looked back and
        mountains
Pierced the air. Snow was formed, this earth
Was gently beginning to live.
We were your fore-runners, we with fins and tails,
With wings and legs. Under the sun we crawled
To life. How good the air was, how sweet the green
Leaves, the rock-pools, the sturdy trees. And flowers

Flaunted such fragrance we wandered among them,
        clung
To their petals or, out of the blue and widespread air,
Descended, drew in our wings and settled where
You now stand or sit or walk. We know
So much about you. We are your family tree
But you have power over us for you can name,
And naming is like possession. It's up to you
To give us our liberty or to make us tame.

Gained

The day is not impoverished any more.
The sun came very late but never mind,
The sky has opened like an unwedged door
And for a moment we are all struck blind,
But blind with happiness. Birds' feathers toss
The air aside, regaining all the loss.

The loss of morning which was quietly grey,
Expectant, but what of? We did not know.
Our disappointment had discarded day
Until this early evening with its show
Of caught-up hours, sun's rising, sunset's glow.

An Event

Legs in knee-socks,
Standing on the rough playground,
Suddenly thinking, 'Why am I here?'

No one else seemed near you,
Though they had been, still were
Except for this awareness.

Long before adolescence
This happened, happened more than once.
Is this the onset

Of that long-travelling,
Never answered
Question, 'Who am I?'

It could be.
The state does not last
But the memory does.

And soon the shouts surround you again.
You have a blue and a red marble in your hand.
It is your turn to roll one.

An Attempt to Charm Sleep

A certain blue
A very dark one
Navy-blue
Going to school
Get back to colour
A pale blue
Somebody's eyes
Or were they grey
Who was the person
Did they like me
Go back to colour
An intolerant blue
A very deep
Inviting water
Is it a river
Where is it going
Shall I swim
What is its name
Go back to colour
Go back to waking
The spell doesn't work
As I stare at the night
It seems like blue

Lullaby

Sleep, my baby, the night is coming soon.
Sleep, my baby, the day has broken down.

Sleep now: let silence come, let the shadows form
A castle of strength for you, a fortress of calm.

You are so small, sleep will come with ease.
Hush now, be still now, join the silences.

At Night

I'm frightened at night
When they put out the light
And the new moon is white.

It isn't so much
That I'm scared stiff to touch
The shadows, and clutch

My blankets: it's – oh –
Things long, long ago
That frighten me so.

If I don't move at all,
The moon will not fall,
There'll be no need to call.

But, strangely, next day
The moon slips away,
The shadows just play.

Vernon Scannell

Vernon Scannell was born in Spilsby, Lincolnshire in 1922, and educated at Queens Park School, Aylesbury, Bucks, and the University of Leeds (1946/7). He served with the Gordon Highlanders in the Second World War, in the Middle East and in Normandy where he was wounded. He lived in many parts of the country, including Wales and Dorset, before returning to Yorkshire in 1980. He has five children.

He has been a boxer, and a teacher of English; but since 1962 he has worked as a freelance writer and broadcaster. His awards for literature include the Heinemann Award (1960) and Cholmondeley Poetry Prize (1974), and he was awarded a Civil List pension for services to literature in 1981. In 1961 he was elected a Fellow of the Royal Society of Literature.

He contributes to many periodicals, and has written books of criticism and numerous radio plays.

His published work includes *A Sense of Danger* (Putnam, 1962); *Walking Wounded* (1965) and *Epithets of War* (1969), both published by Eyre & Spottiswoode; *The Loving Game* (1975), *New and Collected Poems* (1980) and *Winterlude* (1982), all published by Robson; poetry for younger readers, *The Apple Raid and Other Poems* (Chatto & Windus, 1974); and *Mastering the Craft* (Pergamon, 1970). He has written two volumes of autobiography, *The Tiger and the Rose* (Hamish Hamilton, 1971) and *A Proper Gentleman* (Robson, 1977); several novels, and, again for younger readers, *The Dangerous Ones* (Pergamon, 1970) and *A Lonely Game* (Wheaton, 1979). Poems appearing in this collection are taken from *The Apple Raid and Other Poems*, *Epithets of War*, *Mastering the Craft*, *A Sense of Danger*, *Walking Wounded* and unpublished work.

Vernon Scannell has had such a varied and interesting life that it's no wonder he is able, in his writing, to look at different experiences sharply and with understanding. I don't know of any other poet who was once a boxer. Having been a finalist in the Schoolboy Boxing Championship of Great Britain at the age of fourteen, he was later captain of boxing at Leeds University and welter-, middle- and cruiser-weight champion of Northern Universities in 1946/7. He also boxed professionally, and for a short while travelled with a fairground boxing-booth. Boxing seems far removed from poetry, but in his autobiography *The Tiger and the Rose* he writes: 'The boxing contest like the poet's, painter's or composer's struggle with his medium must be conducted within the limits of strict rules, both the artist and the fighter must be dedicated to their tasks.'

Vernon Scannell has always been an avid reader, and as far back as he can remember he wanted to write; but originally poetry held no interest for him. At school it was something you learnt by heart, and often for a punishment. At fifteen years old he came across a second-hand poetry anthology and found himself enjoying the poetry of Thomas Hardy, W. B. Yeats and Walter de la Mare, and, above all, the war poems of Siegfried Sassoon; and suddenly he realized that 'poetry wasn't boring'. This was his beginning.

As well as writing poetry, he has been a tutor on many creative writing courses, gives frequent readings of his own verse, and is a well-known critic and broadcaster. His most recent radio series is called 'A Closer Look', and that's a good title for it. In the programme he delves into different poems, by various poets, with such enthusiasm

[143]

and insight that listeners are inspired to read more themselves.

In his writing I especially enjoy the wry humour that creeps in, and his handling of some of life's less pleasant aspects; failures and fears, anxieties and death. His poetry flows easily, like talking, but never merely rambles; his skill with shape, pattern and language and the surprising ironic twists of mood keep you mentally alert.

Five children of his own, plus experience of teaching, have taught Vernon Scannell that young readers don't want only the 'sweet and prettied' and that they are able to respond to 'truthful, painful and disturbing themes within their own range of experience'. This belief is certainly borne out by those many pupils of mine who, over the years, have asked for 'another poem by Vernon Scannell, please', or 'something as good as *The Apple Raid* or *Hide and Seek*'.

Literature and boxing remain major interests; he also enjoys classical music and walking, is a member of CND and is addicted (like me) to liquorice allsorts.

Poem on Bread

The poet is about to write a poem;
He does not use a pencil or a pen.
He dips his long thin finger into jam
Or something savoury preferred by men.
This poet does not choose to write on paper;
He takes a single slice of well-baked bread
And with his jam or marmite-nibbed forefinger
He writes his verses down on that instead.
His poem is fairly short as all the best are.
When he has finished it he hopes that you
Or someone else – your brother, friend or sister –
Will read and find it marvellous and true.
If you can't read, then eat: it tastes quite good.
If you do neither, all that I can say
Is he who needs no poetry or bread
Is really in a devilish bad way.

View from a High Chair

Here thump on tray
With mug, and splash
Wet white down there.
The sofa purrs,
The window squeaks.
Bump more with mug
And make voice big
Then she will come,
Sky in the room,
Quiet as a cloud,
Flowers in the sky,
Come down snow-soft
But warm as milk,
Hide all the things
That squint with shine,
That gruff and bite
And want to hurt;
Will swallow us
And taste so sweet
As down we go
To try our feet.

Nettles

My son aged three fell in the nettle bed.
'Bed' seemed a curious name for those green spears,
That regiment of spite behind the shed:
It was no place for rest. With sobs and tears
The boy came seeking comfort and I saw
White blisters beaded on his tender skin.
We soothed him till his pain was not so raw.
At last he offered us a watery grin,
And then I took my hook and honed the blade
And went outside and slashed in fury with it
Till not a nettle in that fierce parade
Stood upright any more. Next task: I lit
A funeral pyre to burn the fallen dead.
But in two weeks the busy sun and rain
Had called up tall recruits behind the shed:
My son would often feel sharp wounds again.

Dead Dog

One day I found a lost dog in the street.
The hairs about its grin were spiked with blood,
And it lay still as stone. It must have been
A little dog, for though I only stood
Nine inches for each one of my four years
I picked it up and took it home. My mother
Squealed, and later father spaded out
A bed and tucked my mongrel down in mud.

I can't remember any feeling but
A moderate pity, cool, not swollen-eyed;
Almost a godlike feeling now it seems.
My lump of dog was ordinary as bread.
I have no recollection of the school
Where I was taught my terror of the dead.

Growing Pain

The boy was barely five years old.
We sent him to the little school
And left him there to learn the names
Of flowers in jam jars on the sill
And learn to do as he was told.
He seemed quite happy there until
Three weeks afterwards, at night,
The darkness whimpered in his room.
I went upstairs, switched on his light,
And found him wide awake, distraught,
Sheets mangled and his eiderdown
Untidy carpet on the floor.
I said, 'Why can't you sleep? A pain?'
He snuffled, gave a little moan,
And then he spoke a single word:
'Jessica.' The sound was blurred.
'Jessica? What do you mean?'
'A girl at school called Jessica,
She hurts – ' he touched himself between
The heart and stomach ' – she has been
Aching here and I can see her.'
Nothing I had read or heard
Instructed me in what to do.
I covered him and stroked his head.
'The pain will go, in time,' I said.

The Gift

When Jonathan was almost six years old
He found a most exciting game to play:
The clothes-pegs that his mother kept to hold
The linen chorus firm on washing day
Were not the kind that snap with little jaws
Like tiny crocodiles: her wooden pegs
Were of the type that gypsies make, and more
Fun to play with. Each had two thin legs
To grip the line, a body, small round head
On narrow shoulders. Jonathan began
To play with one, and when his sister said,
'What's that you've got?' he said, 'A wooden man,
A soldier. Look, I've got a regiment.'
For hours, quite happily, he marched and drilled
His wooden army; then he sternly sent
Them out to fight, to triumph or be killed.
His parents watched his game and, for the day
That he was six, they brought him home a treat –
A box of soldiers, some in German grey,
Some in British khaki, all complete
With weapons and equipment. He'd no need
To use those wooden clothes-pegs any more.
He thanked them for his soldiers and agreed
That they were just the troops to wage a war.
They heard him later, marshalling his men;
The noise came from his bedroom. They crept there
To see the joy their present gave him. When
They peeped inside, the sight that met their stare
Amazed them both; for Jonathan had spread
The clothes-pegs on his carpet for the fray;

The birthday gift was packed beneath his bed,
Neat in its box. The parents stole away.
'Why does he still use those?' the father said.
The mother's smile was one that lights and warms:
'Because they have such splendid uniforms.'

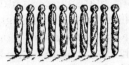

Intelligence Test

'What do you use your eyes for?'
The white-coated man inquired.
'I use my eyes for looking,'
Said Toby, ' – unless I'm tired.'

'I see. And then you close them,'
Observed the white-coated man.
'Well done. A very good answer.
Let's try another one.

'What is your nose designed for?
What use is the thing to you?'
'I use my nose for smelling,'
Said Toby, 'don't you, too?'

'I do indeed,' said the expert,
'That's what the thing is for.
Now I've another question to ask you,
Then there won't be any more.

'What are your ears intended for?
Those things at each side of your head?
Come on – don't be shy – I'm sure you can say.'
'For washing behind,' Toby said.

Uncle Albert

When I was almost eight years old
My Uncle Albert came to stay;
He wore a watch-chain made of gold
And sometimes he would let me play
With both the chain and gleaming watch,
And though at times I might be rough
He never seemed to bother much.
He smelled of shaving soap and snuff,
To me he was a kind of God,
Immensely wise and strong and kind,
And so I thought it rather odd
When I came home from school to find
Two strangers, menacing and tall,
In the parlour, looking grim
As Albert – suddenly quite small –
Let them rudely hustle him
Out to where a black car stood.
Both Albert and his watch and chain
Disappeared that day for good.
My parents said he'd gone to Spain.

Camping Out

His birthday fell in mid-July,
A golden season filled with trees,
Green cauldrons bubbling in the sky
With songs of birds, and, on the breeze
Like airborne petals, butterflies
Signalled, 'Peter now is nine!'

That morning brought a great surprise
Which sent a thrill along his spine
And filled his heart with wordless joy:
His parents gave to him a tent,
A gift that almost any boy
Would welcome, but to him it meant
A dream had wakened into fact –
For months he'd longed to spend a night
Under canvas; all he lacked
Had in a second been put right
When he unpacked his birthday present.
'I'll camp in Coppin's field tonight.'
His father smiled: 'It sounds quite pleasant,
That field's a perfect camping site.
But Peter, out there in the dark
You might be frightened, all alone.
Just now the whole thing seems a lark
But night has terrors of its own.'
Peter laughed and said he knew
That night and day were different;
He felt no fear of darkness. So
As evening fell he pitched his tent
And climbed into his sleeping-bag.

The sun slipped down the west's red throat
And soon the skies began to sag
With weight of blackness, noises float
Eerily in night's dark lake;
Sounds he could not recognize,
Sounds of menace, made him shake,
Sounds that put on strange disguise
As the prowling darkness thickened,
Sounds suggesting hideous forms
Groaned and sighed as heart-beat quickened,
Sounds that spoke of giant worms,
Vampires, demons, scaly beasts.
Peter soon could bear no more;
With chattering teeth he dressed in haste,
Peered once into the dark before
He plunged into the night to flee
On stumbling feet with gasp and moan
Towards the sweet security
That beckoned from his lighted home.

Next day he visited that site
Of freezing horror, but he saw
Nothing of the shapes of night;
The grass was innocent once more,
The petal dance of butterflies
Winked and twinkled, birdsong thrilled
The grateful silence: earth and skies
Wore festive dress, while flowers filled
The air with fragrance and delight;
Each breath he drew seemed like a kiss.
The boy could scarce believe that this
Was where black dread had stalked at night.
Then, dimly, he began to see
That demons, ghosts, and gnomes, and elves
Are necessary fictions we
Mentally create ourselves:
Most monsters die exposed to light
Outside the dark world of the head.
But, all the same, he'd spend tonight
Safe in his warm, familiar bed.

Fear of the Dark

Along the unlit lane on a night
When the stars are blind, the moon masked,
Footsteps follow. I knew a man
Of six foot three who, on dark nights,
Held two lit cigarettes between his lips
Hoping by this bright stratagem
To fox footpads, mislead murderers.
I used to laugh at him, but not now.
I clench teeth and fists and walk fast.
When I reach the house I switch on lights.
The darkness seems defeated, yet
Open the door, the light does not flow far
Beyond the threshold; it stops dead
A few feet from the step, I hear
The darkness growing; it is enormous,
It is in this room in thin disguise.
I am afraid of it, and with good reason.

Hide and Seek

Call out. Call loud: 'I'm ready! Come and find me!'
The sacks in the toolshed smell like the seaside.
They'll never find you in this salty dark,
But be careful that your feet aren't sticking out.
Wiser not to risk another shout.
The floor is cold. They'll probably be searching
The bushes near the swing. Whatever happens
You mustn't sneeze when they come prowling in.
And here they are, whispering at the door;
You've never heard them sound so hushed before.
Don't breathe. Don't move. Stay dumb. Hide in
        your blindness.
They're moving closer, someone stumbles, mutters;
Their words and laughter scuffle, and they're gone.
But don't come out just yet; they'll try the lane
And then the greenhouse and back here again.
They must be thinking that you're very clever,
Getting more puzzled as they search all over.
It seems a long time since they went away.
Your legs are stiff, the cold bites through your coat;
The dark damp smell of sand moves in your throat.
It's time to let them know that you're the winner.
Push off the sacks. Uncurl and stretch. That's better!
Out of the shed and call to them: 'I've won!
Here I am! Come and own up I've caught you!'
The darkening garden watches. Nothing stirs.
The bushes hold their breath; the sun is gone.
Yes, here you are. But where are they who sought
        you?

The Climb and the Dream

The boy had never seen the tree before;
He thought it was a splendid one to climb,
The branches strong enough to take far more
Than his slight weight; and, while they did not
        rhyme
In perfect echoes of each other's shape,
They were arranged in useful patterns which
He found as thrilling as a fire-escape.
Now was his chance! He hopped across the ditch
And wriggled underneath the rusty wire,
And then he found himself confronted by
The lofty challenge, suddenly much higher
Now he was at its foot. He saw the sky
Through foliage and branches, broken like
A pale blue china plate. He leapt and clung
To the lowest branch and swung from left to right,
Then heaved himself astride the swaying rung.
With cautious hands and feet he made a start
From branch to branch; dust tickled in his throat.
He smelt the dark green scent of leaf and bark;
Malicious thorny fingers clutched his coat
And once clawed at his forehead, drawing blood.
Sweat drenched his aching body, blurred his eyes,
But he climbed up and up until he stood
Proud on the highest bough and, with surprise,
Looked down to see the shrunken fields and streams
As if his climb had re-created them;
And he was sure that, often, future dreams
Would bring this vision back to him. But then
A sudden darkening came upon the sky,

He felt the breeze grow burlier and chill,
Joy drained away. And then he realized why:
This was a tree he'd scaled, and not a hill –
The journey down would not be easier
But much more difficult than his ascent:
The foothold surfaces seemed greasier
And less accessible, and he had spent
Much of his strength, was very close to tears,
And sick with fear, yet knew he must go down.
The thing he dreamt about in after-years
Was not the moment when he wore the crown
Of gold achievement on the highest bough
Above the common world of strife and pain,
But the ordeal of dark descent, and how
He sobbed with joy to reach safe earth again.

A Day on the River

It moved so slowly, friendly as a dog
Whose teeth would never bite;
It licked the hand with cool and gentle tongue
And seemed to share its parasites' delight
Who moved upon its back or moored among
The hairy shallows overhung
With natural parasols of leaves
And bubbling birdsong.
Ukuleles twanged and ladies sang
In punts and houseboats vivid as our own
Bold paintings of the Ark;
This was summer's self to any child:
The plop and suck of water and the old
Sweet rankness in the air beguiled
With deft archaic spells the dim
Deliberations of the land,
Dear river, comforting
More than the trailing hand.

The afternoon of sandwiches and flasks
Drifted away.
The breeze across the shivering water grew
Perceptibly in strength. The sun began to bleed.

'Time to go home,' the punctured uncles said,
And back on land
We trembled at the river's faint, low growl
And as birds probed the mutilated sky
We knew that, with the night,
The river's teeth grew sharp,
And they could bite.

The Magic Show

After a feast of sausage-rolls,
Sandwiches of various meats,
Jewelled jellies, brimming bowls
Of chocolate ice and other treats,
We children played at Blind Man's Buff,
Hide-and-Seek, Pin-the-Tail-on-Ned,
And then – when we'd had just enough
Of party games – we all were led
Into another room to see
The Magic Show. The wizard held
A wand of polished ebony;
His white-gloved, flickering hands compelled
The rapt attention of us all.
He conjured from astonished air
A living pigeon and a fall
Of paper snowflakes; made us stare
Bewildered, as a playing card –
Unlike a leopard – changed its spots
And disappeared. He placed some starred
And satin scarves in silver pots,
Withdrew them as plain bits of rag,
Then swallowed them before our eyes.
But soon we felt attention flag
And found delighted, first surprise
Had withered like a wintry leaf;
And, when the tricks were over, we
Applauded, yet felt some relief,
And left the party willingly.
'Good night', we said, 'and thank you for
The lovely time we've had.' Outside

The freezing night was still. We saw
Above our heads the slow clouds stride
Across the vast, unswallowable skies;
White, graceful gestures of the moon,
The stars intent and glittering eyes,
And, gleaming like a silver spoon,
The frosty path to lead us home.
Our breath hung blossoms on unseen
Boughs of air as we passed there,
And we forgot that we had been
Pleased briefly by that conjuror,
Could not recall his tricks, or face,
Bewitched and awed, as now we were,
By magic of the commonplace.

A Question of Faith

When I was in the top class in the school
Science was added to the syllabus
Of History, English, Arithmetic and Geog.
Our teacher, Archie Dawson, bald as chalk,
Did tricks with a magnet and some iron stubble,
Talked of magnetic fields and molecules,
Gave the rainbow a ghostly name; my brain began
    to clog.
I gave up trying to follow; just sat in my private fog.

And then we did an experiment. Each of us brought
An empty jam-jar to school. We were going to make
A Leclanché cell. (To me it sounded far
More like a dungeon in the Bastille than what
It was: a primitive electric battery.)
Into each jar old Archie poured some acid
And each one of us was given a zinc and copper bar:
These we immersed in the acid in the jar.

'Now,' said Archie, 'when you get your wires
Fix one to each of the two bars in the acid
And then you'll find these bulbs I'm handing out
Will light up when the circuit is completed.'
There was a pause of lip-chewed concentration,
Then seconds later voices flashed out loud:
'Hey look! It works!' And this delighted shout
Was multiplied. I felt familiar doubt

As, carefully, I joined the wires to my two bars
And then attached them to the flashlamp bulb.
It stayed egg white. 'Please, sir, mine won't react!'
'What's that? The bulb must be a dud. Use this,
This one's all right. I've tried it out myself.'
He snuffled off, later came back: 'All right?'
I nodded. 'Yes, sir, thanks.' But this was not a fact.
The bulb stayed white and blind. It was faith that I lacked.

Incendiary

That one small boy with a face like pallid cheese
And burnt-out little eyes could make a blaze
As brazen, fierce and huge, as red and gold
And zany yellow as the one that spoiled
Three thousand guineas' worth of property
And crops at Godwin's Farm on Saturday
Is frightening – as fact and metaphor:
An ordinary match intended for
The lighting of a pipe or kitchen fire
Misused may set a whole menagerie
Of flame-fanged tigers roaring hungrily.
And frightening, too, that one small boy should set
The sky on fire and choke the stars to heat
Such skinny limbs and such a little heart
Which would have been content with one warm kiss
Had there been anyone to offer this.

House for Sale

The wind is loud, wraps noise about the house;
Night is a dark factory making sounds.
Outside the town, the last few trees plead,
Begging reprieve, but find they have no grounds.

Here, the walls are crumbling, windows tremble;
A new crack has spidered over the plaster;
The house should be disposed of before it falls down,
But who, in his right mind, would be its master?

Above this varicosed ceiling the children sleep;
Restlessly they mutter in the house's brain;
The eldest has a bag packed, ready, under the bed,
Will leave tomorrow on an early train.

Washing Day

Suds twinkle, weightless diamonds,
Glittering seeds of bled pomegranates.
Beneath the airy coruscations
The water is blue, diluted ink.
Steam sweetens the kitchen's breath,
Windows grow thoughtful, dream.
Sheets and shirts are punched and squeezed,
Wrung out and dumped
Heavy like lumps of dough
Into a dry tub,
Are heaved into the sun and hung
Uncurled on a windy sky
To ripple and swell, swank and flap:
Hygienic bunting, a celebration
Of victory, ephemeral but real.

Cat

My cat has got no name,
We simply call him Cat;
He doesn't seem to blame
Anyone for that.

For he is not like us
Who often, I'm afraid,
Kick up quite a fuss
If *our* names are mislaid.

As if, without a name,
We'd be no longer there
But like a tiny flame
Vanish in bright air.

My pet, he doesn't care
About such things as that:
Black buzz and golden stare
Require no name but Cat.

Hearthquake

A week has passed without a word being said:
No headlines, though that's natural, I suppose
Since there were no injured, let alone dead,
Yet I expected a paragraph or so.
But no, not even comment passed in bars,
No gossip over fences while shirts flap
And sheets boast on the line like sails on spars,
And yet it happened: I can swear to that.
I remember it as if it were last night,
My sitting smug and cosy as a cat
Until the carpet suddenly took fright
And bucked beneath my feet. Walls winced. The
     clock
Upon the mantelpiece began to dance;
The photograph of me aged twenty-one fell flat;
Glass cracked. The air went cold with shock.
I did not sleep at all well through that night
Nor have I since. I cannot understand
Why no one – not my nearest neighbour even –
Refers to what occurred on that strange evening
Unless, in some way difficult to see,
He is afraid to mention it. Like me.

Moods of Rain

It can be so tedious, a bore
Telling a long dull story you have heard before
So often it is meaningless;
Yet, in another mood,
It comes swashbuckling, swishing a million foils,
Feinting at daffodils, peppering tin pails,
Pelting so fast on roof, umbrella, hood,
You hear long silk being torn;
Refurbishes old toys, and oils
Slick surfaces that gleam as if unworn.
Sometimes a cordial summer rain will fall
And string on railings delicate small bells;
Soundless as seeds on soil
Make green ghosts rise.
It can be fierce, hissing like blazing thorns,
Or side-drums hammering at night-filled eyes
Until you wake and hear a long grief boil
And, overflowing, sluice
The lost raft of the world.
Yet it can come as lenitive and calm
As comfort from the mother of us all
Sighing you into sleep
Where peace prevails and only soft rains fall.

Uncle Edward's Affliction

Uncle Edward was colour-blind;
We grew accustomed to the fact.
When he asked someone to hand him
The green book from the window-seat
And we observed its bright red cover
Either apathy or tact
Stifled comment. We passed it over.
Much later, I began to wonder
What curious world he wandered in,
Down streets where pea-green pillar-boxes
Grinned at a fire-engine as green;
How Uncle Edward's sky at dawn
And sunset flooded marshy green.
Did he ken John Peel with his coat so green
And Robin Hood in Lincoln Red?
On country walks avoid being stung
By nettles hot as a witch's tongue?
What meals he savoured with his eyes:
Green strawberries and fresh red peas,
Green beef and greener burgundy.
All unscientific, so it seems:
His world was not at all like that,
So those who claim to know have said.
Yet, I believe, in war-smashed France
He must have crawled from neutral mud
To lie in pastures dark and red
And seen, appalled, on every blade
The rain of innocent green blood.

November Story

The evening had caught cold;
Its eyes were blurred.
It had a dripping nose
And its tongue was furred.

I sat in a warm bar
After the day's work;
November snuffled outside,
Greasing the sidewalk.

But soon I had to go
Out into the night
Where shadows prowled the alleys,
Hiding from the light.

But light shone at the corner
On the pavement where
A man had fallen over
Or been knocked down there.

His legs on the slimed concrete
Were splayed out wide;
He had been propped against a lamp-post;
His head lolled to one side.

A victim of crime or accident,
An image of fear,
He remained quite motionless
As I drew near.

Then a thin voice startled silence
From a doorway close by
Where an urchin hid from the wind:
'Spare a penny for the guy!'

I gave the boy some money
And hastened on.
A voice called, 'Thank you guv'nor!'
And the words upon

The wincing air seemed strange –
So hoarse and deep –
As if the guy had spoken
In his restless sleep.

Death of a Snowman

I was awake all night,
Big as a polar bear,
Strong and firm and white.
The tall black hat I wear
Was draped with ermine fur.
I felt so fit and well
Till the world began to stir
And the morning sun swell.
I was tired, began to yawn;
At noon in the humming sun
I caught a severe warm;
My nose began to run.
My hat grew black and fell,
Was followed by my grey head.
There was no funeral bell,
But by tea-time I was dead.

Snow Dream

He walked upon the silent quilt of snow:
Night, a buried moon and all the stars
Swept away like cinders while the slow
Sewing of the flakes performed their dance
In spectral trillions, musicless pavan.
He was alone in the night of endless snow,
The world's most lonely, maybe its only man.
Behind, each footprint instantly filled in;
He left no trail, there was no path to follow.
If he began his own snowdance – to spin
Tranced pirouettes – when still, he would not know
Which way led forward, which would take him back.
He would not know which way he ought to go.
But neither did he now – no guide, no track,
Moonslaughter done and every star stone dead –
He drifted through the white storm in his head,
The ceaseless cancellation of the snow.

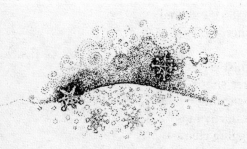

from *First Fight*

BITE ON GUMSHIELD

Bite on gumshield,
Guard held high,
The crowd are silenced,
All sounds die.
Lead with the left,
Again, again;
Watch for the opening,
Feint and then
Hook to the body
But he's blocked it and
Slammed you back
With a fierce right hand.
Hang on grimly,
The fog will clear,
Sweat in your nostrils,
Grease and fear.
You're hurt and staggering,
Shocked to know
That the story's altered:
He's the hero!

But the mist is clearing,
The referee snaps
A rapid warning
And he smartly taps
Your hugging elbow
And then you step back
Ready to counter

[177]

The next attack,
But the first round finishes
Without mishap.
You suck in the air
From the towel's skilled flap.
A voice speaks urgently
Close to your ear:
'Keep your left going, Boy,
Stop him getting near.
He wants to get close to you,
So jab him off hard;
When he tries to slip below,
Never mind your guard,
Crack him with a solid right,
Hit him on the chin,
A couple downstairs
And then he'll pack it in.'

Slip in the gumshield
Bite on it hard,
Keep him off with your left,
Never drop your guard.
Try a left hook,
But he crosses with a right
Smack on your jaw
And Guy Fawkes' Night
Flashes and dazzles
Inside your skull,
Your knees go bandy
And you almost fall.
Keep the left jabbing,
Move around the ring,
Don't let him catch you with

Another hook or swing.
Keep your left working,
Keep it up high,
Stab it out straight and hard,
Again – above the eye.
Sweat in the nostrils,
But nothing now of fear,
You're moving smooth and confident
In comfortable gear.
Jab with the left again,
Quickly move away;
Feint and stab another in,
See him duck and sway.
Now for the pay-off punch,
Smash it hard inside;
It thuds against his jaw, he falls,
Limbs spread wide.
And suddenly you hear the roar,
Hoarse music of the crowd,
Voicing your hot ecstasy,
Triumphant, male and proud.

*

Now, in the sleepless darkness of his room
The Boy, in bed, remembers. Suddenly
The victory tastes sour. The man he fought
Was not a thing, as lifeless as a broom,
He was a man who hoped and trembled too;
What of him now? What was *he* going through?
And then The Boy bites hard on resolution:
Fighters can't pack pity with their gear,
And yet a bitter taste stays with the notion;
He's forced to swallow down one treacherous tear.

But that's the last. He is a boy no longer;
He is a man, a fighter, such as jeer
At those who make salt beads with melting eyes,
Whatever might cry out, is hurt, or dies.

I Bit an Apple . . .

I bit an apple and the flesh was sweet:
Juice tingled on the tongue and from the fruit
Arose a scent that memory received
And in a flash raised ghosts of apple trees,
Leaves blistered with minutest bulbs of rain
Bewildering an autumn drawing-room
Where carpets stained with unaccustomed shadow
Heard one old table creak, perhaps moved too
By some remembrance of a former time
When summer like a lover came to him
And laid amazing offerings at his feet.
I bit an apple and the spell was sweet.

The Apple-raid

Darkness came early, though not yet cold;
Stars were strung on the telegraph wires;
Street lamps spilled pools of liquid gold;
The breeze was spiced with garden fires.

That smell of burnt leaves, the early dark,
Can still excite me but not as it did
So long ago when we met in the park –
Myself, John Peters and David Kidd.

We moved out of town to the district where
The lucky and wealthy had their homes
With garages, gardens, and apples to spare
Clustered in the trees' green domes.

We chose the place we meant to plunder
And climbed the wall and tip-toed through
The secret dark. Apples crunched under
Our feet as we moved through the grass and dew.

We found the lower boughs of a tree
That were easy to reach. We stored the fruit
In pockets and jerseys until all three
Boys were heavy with their tasty loot.

Safe on the other side of the wall
We moved back to town and munched as we went.
I wonder if David remembers at all
That little adventure, the apples' fresh scent.

Strange to think that he's fifty years old,
That tough little boy with scabs on his knees;
Stranger to think that John Peters lies cold
In an orchard in France beneath apple trees.

John Walsh

John Walsh was born in July 1911 in Brighton, Sussex, and spent his early years there, later moving to Otford, near Sevenoaks, Kent, and finally to Alfriston, in Sussex.

He went to Varndean School, Brighton, and then read English at University College, London, where he was a scholar of his college. He became a teacher, and was head of the English Department at Chislehurst and Sidcup Grammar School. As well as teaching and writing, he was assistant editor of the quarterly *The Use of English*.

His published work includes *The Roundabout by the Sea* (Oxford University Press, 1960), *The Truants* (1965) and *The House in the Cedar Tree* (1966), both published by Heinemann, and a collection of children's writing, *Fields of Experience* (Heinemann Educational, 1968). Many of his poems have been broadcast on BBC Radio for Schools and appeared in the magazines *Stories and Rhymes*, *Living Language* and *Poetry Corner*. John Walsh married and had one son and one daughter. He died in 1972.

Poems in this collection are taken from *The Roundabout by the Sea*, *The Truants* and unpublished work.

It must have been about twelve years ago that I first came across John Walsh's poem 'I've Got an Apple Ready', and it took me back to my childhood, reminding me of how I was once scared by a bullying boy. When, a little later, I read 'The Bully Asleep', and saw how subtly he described the sad side of that same bully, I knew that here was a writer who could write for and about children with understanding and without sentimentality. I looked for more of his work, and liked it. The children I taught liked it too, because it was about the things they knew and recognized, and yet was never dull; through his writing they looked at ordinary incidents in a different way.

John Walsh wrote of what he knew first-hand and so his poems have a feel of everyday happenings, real experiences; they are set in schoolrooms, in houses, on beaches. His own two children appear frequently: Catherine, his daughter, *did* deal with the real Mouser's fleas as the girl does in 'Marjorie Sitting on the Doorstep'. His son, Patrick, when aged three, *did* pick quantities of dandelions and spread the juice down his clean white blouse, just like the baby in 'Taking Out Jim'. He had the ability to turn the small incidents of home life, and his teaching days, into poetry.

He was a man who worked hard but enjoyed his leisure time, too. Walking, especially over the Sussex Downs, gave him great pleasure; he knew where to find newts and the first violets of spring. He was an excellent cook, and loved preparing food for family and friends and his older pupils who were often invited for meals. This kind of informal entertaining was much more to his taste than formal occasions and smart parties. After supper he would play records: his favourite music was by Haydn, Mozart, Wagner, Elgar and Fauré; he didn't care for Bach. His music collection gradually diminished because of his generous habit of giving records away to any boy who showed interest.

He had an extraordinary memory and was able to quote poems and whole scenes from Shakespeare by heart; very useful for an English teacher, and someone with such love of words. In his own writing he cared deeply about good craftsmanship, and would correct and re-correct until he felt satisfied.

Although for a great deal of his life John Walsh struggled against ill health, he never allowed it to spoil his enjoyment of teaching or his relationships with people. Long after they had left school, his pupils remembered his sense of humour and the stories he made up for them. He was known affectionately as 'the funniest master we ever had'.

His wife, Mary, and his family said that 'living with him was tremendous fun and an intense enjoyment. The world was very different seen through his eyes.'

This selection would no doubt have surprised a man who was always modest about his own success and amazed if recognition came his way. I hope he would have been pleased too. I don't think he had the recognition he truly deserved, as a children's poet, during his lifetime.

'I've Got an Apple Ready'

My hair's tightly plaited;
I've a bright blue bow;
I don't want my breakfast,
And now I must go.

My satchel's on my shoulder;
Nothing's out of place;
And I've got an apple ready,
Just in case.

So it's 'Good-bye, Mother!'
And off down the street;
Briskly at first
On pit-a-pat feet,

But slow and more slow
As I reach the tarred
Trackway that runs
By Hodson's Yard;

For it's there sometimes
Bill Craddock waits for me
To snatch off my beret
And throw it in a tree.

Bill Craddock leaning
On Hodson's rails;
Bill with thin hands
And dirty nails;

Bill with a front tooth
Broken and bad;
His dark eyes cruel,
And somehow sad.

Often there are workmen,
And then he doesn't dare;
But this morning I feel
He'll be there.

At the corner he will pounce . . .
But quickly I'll say
'Hallo, Bill! have an apple!' –
In an ordinary way.

I'll push it in his hand
And walk right on;
And when I'm round the corner
I'll run!

The New Boy

The door swung inward. I stood and breathed
The new-school atmosphere:
The smell of polish and disinfectant,
And the flavour of my own fear.

I followed into the cloakroom; the walls
Rang to the shattering noise
Of boys who barged and boys who banged;
Boys and still more boys!

A boot flew by me. Its angry owner
Pursued with force and yell;
Somewhere a man snapped orders; somewhere
There clanged a warning bell.

And there I hung with my new schoolmates;
They pushing and shoving me; I
Unknown, unwanted, pinned to the wall;
On the verge of ready-to-cry.

Then, from the doorway, a boy called out:
'Hey, you over there! You're new!
Don't just stand there propping the wall up!
I'll look after you!'

I turned; I timidly raised my eyes;
He stood and grinned meanwhile;
And my fear died, and my lips answered
Smile for his smile.

He showed me the basins, the rows of pegs;
He hung my cap at the end;
He led me away to my new classroom ...
And now that boy's my friend.

From the Classroom Window

Sometimes, when heads are deep in books,
And nothing stirs,
The sunlight touches that far hill,
And its three dark firs;
Then on those trees I fix my eyes –
And teacher hers.

Together awhile we contemplate
The air-blue sky
And those dark tree-tops; till, with a tiny
Start and sigh,
She turns again to the printed page –
And so do I.

But our two thoughts have met out there
Where no school is –
Where, among call of birds and faint
Shimmer of bees,
They rise in sunlight, resinous, warm –
Those dark fir-trees!

The Truants

So I cried 'We will!' and Roy echoed 'We will!'
And he snatched the cap from his head;
And we swung our bicycles away from the school
    gates,
And made off for the hills instead;

Being maddened by the wind of a brisk March
    morning,
And the tang of a clear March sun,
And the thought of the walls, the desks, the dismal
    faces,
And the homework we'd left undone.

We thrust our caps in our bicycle-bags, along with
Our gym-shoes, sandwiches, books;
And we rode hard with determined faces, avoiding
The policeman's furrowed looks.

We pushed up on to the turf – the stubbly grass
Zinging our bicycle-rims;
Five-past nine! And above, the dizzying larks
Reeled off their air-blue hymns!

On the windless side of a dry thorn, an adder
Was crept to taste the sun;
He felt our presence a stealthy moment – and then
With a soft slither was gone.

So on to the bare hill's crest, where we sat at last,
Unpacked, and swapped our food;
Never on dry bruised turf, scented in sunlight,
Had sandwiches tasted so good.

All morning we gossiped – joked about this and that,
(Though not about home or school);
And later, in the beech-copse, where the warm sun-
    shadows
Fell twiggy and cool,

I found some pale white violets, their scent brimming
A heart suddenly glad;
And I said 'I shall pick a bunch for my mother',
    but didn't –
For the thought of her made me sad.

So noon shifted to afternoon; and the warmth
Came fainter, the air more keen;
Yet still we sprawled on the turf, and still we chatted,
With silences in between.

Till I said 'Let's go!' and Roy echoed 'Let's go!'
The day had clouded; the sun
Dropped early (it seemed) from the sky, and with
    it the larks
Dropped earthward one by one.

And soon we were following the townward road
    – myself
With Roy tagging behind;
And a last lark sank, singing, singing, into the
Darkness of my own mind.

For the glory was over: in the dusk, two truant
      schoolboys
Were wending their sad way home;
Slow and more slow; guilty; and oh! with a sickening
Sense of the trouble to come!

Paul's Flowers

The clock said two; the iron
School-bell had ceased to clank,
When Paul lingered to pick
Three dandelions on the bank.

No children in the school yard;
None by the gate.
He pushed the class-door open
And saw that he was late.

All eyed him. Paul came forward
With hesitating foot,
Laid his three flowers in teacher's
Lap and was mute.

Then in the shocked stillness
Teacher began to scold. . . .
But Paul, his eyes turned downward
To her dress's fold,
Saw those three flowers had grown
To a strange gold.

Strange gold that breathed a petalled
Warmth on the air!
And one black midge that basked
In summer there!

With shut ears Paul watched it –
Shut ears and bended head –
Till teacher's voice had faded;
And, 'Take your flowers!' she said.

Paul to his desk has gone,
Silent, and on his knee
Holding the three bright dandelions
Miserably.

The Bully Asleep

One afternoon, when grassy
Scents through the classroom crept,
Bill Craddock laid his head
Down on his desk, and slept.

The children came round him:
Jimmy, Roger, and Jane;
They lifted his head timidly
And let it sink again.

'Look, he's gone sound asleep, Miss,'
Said Jimmy Adair;
'He stays up all the night, you see;
His mother doesn't care.'

'Stand away from him, children.'
Miss Andrews stooped to see.
'Yes, he's asleep; go on
With your writing, and let him be.'

'Now's a good chance!' whispered Jimmy;
And he snatched Bill's pen and hid it.
'Kick him under the desk, hard;
He won't know who did it.'

'Fill all his pockets with rubbish –
Paper, apple-cores, chalk.'
So they plotted, while Jane
Sat wide-eyed at their talk.

Not caring, not hearing,
Bill Craddock he slept on;
Lips parted, eyes closed –
Their cruelty gone.

'Stick him with pins!' muttered Roger.
'Ink down his neck!' said Jim.
But Jane, tearful and foolish,
Wanted to comfort him.

On These November Evenings

On these November evenings
We walk home quietly.
The others call, 'Good-bye, Ann!'
And hurry indoors for tea.

But David and I run out
To sit on the rails
And watch the passing traffic
Until the light fails.

We watch the heavy lorries,
Each with its swinging load
Of rods and iron piping,
Move down the by-pass road.

David on the bus-stop railing
Does antics, crying, 'Ann,
Can you do backward-twizzles?'
Of course I can!

Sometimes a shouting gipsy,
Her face hard and sour,
Goes by, drops from her basket
A chrysanthemum flower.

And sometimes Ted and Alan
Come running. They can't wait:
They're off to meet their father
Outside the factory gate.

Or John and Betty Savage.
'Down to the shop!' cries John.
'See you at pictures tomorrow!'
And they both hurry on.

We wait. The yellow vapour
Which has warmed the air all day
Thickens into a darkness
Over the River Cray.

Till all at once the road-lamps
Shine white overhead;
And David's face beneath them
Is weird and ghastly-dead.

'Look, Dave! The factory-windows!
Don't all the lights look gold?'
But David he sits quiet;
And the rail grows cold.

We watch the moving head-lamps.
And now in the long line
There comes the lighted number
Of a 3-2-9.

It slides to a standstill:
The workmen push and shout,
Struggling past the conductor
To be first out.

Then a sudden voice says, 'Hallo, dear!'
And from the throbbing bus
Gets Mother, with her smile and her basket,
And a cake for us!

Last Day of the Summer Term

We sit around in the classroom
Exchanging holiday plans;
The many familiar faces –
Kate's and Maud's and Anne's!

Kate's spending a month in Brighton;
Joan is for Paris; Maud's
Going to an aunt in Scotland,
And Anne to the Norfolk Broads.

I listen, envious and silent,
Or do the jobs of the day:
Tidy up; stack books; or I read
In a half-hearted sort of way.

We gather for the last Assembly –
The prayers and the final hymn;
'If you girls go on being fidgety
I shall keep the whole school in.'

But it's over at last, all over;
And I walk along home with Sue,
And stand at her door, while she chatters
About what they're going to do:

They've hired a holiday-caravan
Down on the Isle of Wight:
'We shall set out by car this evening –
We'll be travelling all night . . .

'Ah, well! Good-bye till September!'
I go on to my house alone;
I find my key, and enter
My holiday-home.

The house is close and quiet;
A few dead roses spill
Their petals one by one
On the hot window-sill.

A tap drips in the kitchen;
Two flies buzz on the pane;
There's a note on the breakfast-table:
Two lines from Mother. – 'Dear Jane,

'Make yourself a cup of tea, dear;
I'll be working late at the shop.'
And I turn with hardly a sigh
To the uncleared washing-up;

Or wander vaguely upstairs,
To stare awhile at the tall
Unanswering photo of father
That hangs on my bedroom wall.

Waving at Trains

Down in the dandelion-field,
Watching the holiday trains go by,
All afternoon we waited,
Billy and I.
Train after train after train –
There were twenty at least, we reckoned;
But hardly a head turned round, and no one gave
The answering wave;
And we gradually lost all hope,
And our hands slackened.

Just one more train . . .

It came, slowly climbing the slope:
On cushioned seats the holiday-people sat;
They read their papers, smoked and chatted and ate;
The train swept by, solemn and grand.
Then, at the very last,
(The train was almost past),
Suddenly, there at the window, a face leaned out –
And look! a smile, a wave, a fluttering hand!

Till that train was out of sight,
We waved, Billy and I did –
We waved with all our might.

Down to the Sea

Our train stopped short; and over the fields
The children came,
Leaving their house of hay; running,
With cheeks aflame,

To cling and perch on the trackside railing –
To wave and stare:
Envying me my rockety ride
To the salt sea air.

And I waved too, and was waving still
When we moved away,
And quietly over the fields they went
To their house of hay.

Our train sped on; but left my envious
Thoughts with them there –
Wanting their play, their fields of sunshine,
And the poppies in their hair!

The Arrival

Our train steams slowly in, and we creep to a stop
    at last.
There's a great unlatching of doors, and the coaches,
    emptying fast,
Let loose their loads of children, and mothers with
    talkative friends,
And sandwiches, flasks and push-chairs, and apples,
    and odds and ends.

And we move in a crowd together, amid churns and
    trolleys and crates,
Along by a cobbled courtyard, and out through the
    station gates;
We pass by the waiting taxis; then turn a corner and
    reach
To where with its flags and cafés the road curves
    down to the beach.

We move in the livelier air, between shining shops
    and stalls;
Never was such a confusion of coloured, bright
    beach-balls,
And plastic buckets and boats, and ducks of a
    rubbery blue,
And strings of sandals, and stacks of rock-with-the-
    name-right-through!

Till the many smells which beset us – of onions
    and cooking greens,
Of fumes from the cars and buses, of smoke from the
    noisy inns –

All merge in the one large gust which blows on us
    broad and free,
And catches us, throat, and limbs, and heart – the
    smell of the sea!

Beach Burial

Yes, but lay yourself down
In this hollow and pebbly nest;
I take the small stones, so,
And gently on arms and breast
I pile them – the salty stones
Which the sun has warmed and dried.
Be still; the sea's far out.
No fear of the returning tide.

Three more stones and it's done:
Your shoulders, hands, and clothes
By a pebbly mound are hidden,
And the obstinate, peeping toes.
The pebbles circle your chin;
Of your hair and ears not a trace;
And I stand, looking gravely down
On your upward, smiling face.

The Sand Castle

All evening I worked to build me a huge
Castle of sand;
While the gulls' cry and the sea's cry
Drew back from the land.

I toiled and toiled; till there, by the light
Of the hard moon,
A fortress stood, black-shadowed, grim,
Triumphant ... Soon

They came to fetch me. 'Come now, Jeremy,
It's supper,' they said;
And 'No more play tonight, Jeremy –
It's time for bed.'

But here I'll watch by my bedroom window,
Cold-footed, alone,
Till the full sea comes shining in –
And my castle's gone.

Blind Boy on the Shore

Set down by himself on the sandy shore,
Unseeing, as if asleep,
He dug at once with his new spade;
And, heap after little heap,

He filled and emptied his pail, groping
Each time with steady hand,
And sensitive fingers' touch, to test
The shape of the moulded sand.

But little by little his work slackened;
He sat with uplifted spade,
And listened instead to the far sea,
And the cries of children who played.

Then, from close by, there came the quiet
Singing of a younger child . . .
He dug no more, but gave up gently,
Lay back in the sun, and smiled.

Shadows on Bantwick Sand

Still morning!
The first faint breakfast-smells
From the long line of Bantwick shore-hotels
Come beachward to find me;
And I stand
Alone on Bantwick sand,
And as the sun broadens behind me,
My long black shadow runs flatly out –
Out to the sea and the far rocks,
Where the fishermen lift their lobster-pots,
Their boats quietly chugging
In the still morning.

. . .

Cool evening!
Out in the bay, by the far rocks,
Where the fishermen bait their lobster-pots,
The broad sun sends its level rays
Shoreward to blind me;
And I stand
Alone on Bantwick sand,
And my shadow unrolls behind me:

Back to the land it stretches
A dark finger, and reaches
To the old stone house where we've always stayed,
Where the windows are open, the savoury dishes
    ready,
The silver, the white cloth laid –
In the cool evening.

The Roundabout by the Sea

The crimson-spotted horses,
Long-tailed and glassy-eyed,
With feet outstretched before them
Go circling side by side;
Rising,
Falling,
In slow unthinking play –
All day.

On hoofs for ever silent
They climb or dip the air;
Some with their clinging riders,
Some riderless and bare;
Rising,
Falling,
With flash of bridles gay –
All day.

The old man turns his handle:
The horses creak and glide.
No other sound, no music
But the music of the tide,
Rising,
Falling,
In pebbled wash and spray –
All day.

All day.

Journey Home

I remember the long homeward ride, begun
By the light that slanted in from the level sun;
And on the far embankment, in sunny heat,
Our whole train's shadow travelling, dark and
    complete.

A farmer snored. Two loud gentlemen spoke
Of the cricket and news. The pink baby awoke
And gurgled awhile. Till slowly out of the day
The last light sank in glimmer and ashy-grey.

I remember it all; and dimly remember, too,
The place where we changed – the dark trains
    lumbering through;
The refreshment-room, the crumbs and the slopped
    tea;
And the salt on my face, not of tears, not tears,
    but the sea.

Our train at last! Said father, 'Now tumble in!
It's the last lap home!' And I wondered what 'lap'
    could mean;
But the rest is all lost, for a huge drowsiness crept
Like a yawn upon me; I leant against Mother and
    slept.

The House That Jack Built

The reaping-machine was gone, and the straw was
     in blocks again:
Huge oblong blocks of straw under a rainy sky –
New straw, smelling like apples under the soft rain.
We jumped from our bikes, Bob and Billy and I –
Ran into the field, and started to heave and haul,
Dragging the huge straw blocks to make a roughly-
     shaped wall.
'Anything, anything,' I shouted, 'to get into the dry!'
And we piled them one on top of the other,
Hoisting them higgledy-piggledy high.

It had rained gently at first;
Now, in a moment, the clouds burst,
And the storm which all day had threatened
     suddenly broke;
The thunder bellowed; the lightning
Went zagging across the sky in fiery reds,
And the rain gushed down.
'Hold tight, everybody!' I cried. 'We're in for a soak!'
And we jerked our jerseys over our heads,
And laboured on.

Till at last Bob cried,
'Drop it now, Jack – we've done enough!'
For a second we eyed
Our house with pride –
Three shaky walls, and a crooked sort of a roof.
Then we knelt on the earth and dived thankfully
     under;

Who cares now for rain, lightning and thunder?
We are safe – safe –
Safe in our snug and strawy den!

But then ... but then ... *oh, then!*
We were just beginning to lark and play,
When there came a lurch and a sway,
And the walls with a sudden swish gave way –
And the whole stack
Came down on top of us,
Buried the lot of us –
Bill on his side, Bob on his face, me on the flat of
     my back!
Poor Bill! Poor Bob!

Poor Jack!

The Swing

The garden-swing at the lawn's edge
Is hung beneath the hawthorn-hedge;
White branches droop above, and shed
Their petals on the swinger's head.
Here, now the day is almost done,
And leaves are pierced by the last sun,
I sit where hawthorn-breezes creep
Round me, and swing the hours to sleep:
Swinging alone –
By myself alone –
Alone,
Alone,
Alone.

In a soft shower the hawthorn-flakes descend.
Dusk falls at last. The dark-leaved branches bend
Earthward . . . The longest dream must have an end.

Now in my bedroom half-undressed,
My face against the window pressed,
I see once more the things which day
Gave me, and darkness takes away:
The garden-path still dimly white,
The lawn, the flower-beds sunk in night,
And, brushed by some uncertain breeze,
A ghostly swing beneath ghostly trees:
Swinging alone –
By itself alone –
Alone,
Alone,
Alone.

Joan Who Hates Parties

Today's little Doreen's party-day;
And it all begins when I'm snatched from play
By Mother, who cries with a gay little laugh,
'Now come along first and have a nice bath!'
And off come my jeans and I'm dumped straight in,
And splashed all over from toes to chin;
Then dumped out again on the big bath-mat –
And don't I just hate that!

For the next half-hour I am rubbed rough-dry,
And tickled with talc till I'm ready to cry,
And perched half-dressed on a backless chair
For the fight between Mother and me and my hair;
Then on go the shoes and the clean white socks,
And the dreamiest of dream-like nylon frocks,
With a sweet blue bow for the end of my plait –
And don't I just hate that!

But I'm ready at last; and at ten-past four
I'll be dropped at dear little Doreen's door;
And at Doreen's door I'll be met with a hearty
Welcome to dear little Doreen's party;

But they won't see me – they won't see Joan –
But a girl with a heart like a thunder-stone;
A girl with the face of a fierce tom-cat . . .
And won't they just hate that!

'Good Night, Mouser!'

'Good night, Mouser!'

The front door closes,
The bolt slides home,
And Mouser hops down into the garden,
A cat unwanted, alone.

The late-night neighbour,
Hurrying along
Click-clack on the empty street,
Feels a sudden fur at his feet.
Wondering he bends,
And Mouser winds about him,
Furring him,
Purring him
Most pleadingly,
For even in the dark, Mouser knows all his friends.
But the neighbour rises and feels for his key:
'Good night, Mouser!
Run away now and play!'
And Mouser wanders away.

All the long night he'll stray
Through empty garden, or waste and thorny patch,
Nosing at a pebble or a snail
In the flower-bed;
His ears straining to catch
The squeak of a fallen fledgling, not yet dead;
His paw ready to snatch
At the scuttering rat,

Or the beaded mouse with the flickering tail.
All the long night, prowling and prying,
Around the cold roots of the thorns;
Or sometimes just lying
In a tuft of grass,
Just lying in wait, no more.

But when daylight dawns
He is back at the door –
Back with his doorstep offering of rat or mouse;
And he sits with uplifted chin,
Endlessly patient, watching the house,
Watching for the twitch of the curtain,
Waiting for the slide of the bolt,
And the voice that cries, 'Come in!'

Stay in tonight, Mouser!
Quick, up the stairs before others can see!
No longer alone,
NOT a cat-without-a-home,
Stay warm in my bed with me!

Marjorie Sitting on the Doorstep

Marjorie, sitting on the doorstep,
Grips Mouser between her knees,
And dusts his coat to keep away
The harvesters and fleas.
And Mouser, quiet at first,
Quickly forgets to purr
When the white powder is sprinkled and rubbed
Into his black fur.
He snarls, spits, struggles, and bites –
Would wriggle out if he could;
While Marjorie laughs, 'Keep still, Mouser!
It's all for your own good!'
Chest, neck and ears, no inch is spared;
Till at last, when all is ended,
He leaps away with a mighty start;
And now he sits, hump-backed, apart,
A Mouser grey and offended!

Winter Birds

From the sofa'd room
In warm firelight
We looked on a garden
Freezing white,

And saw how the sparrows
In flocks below
Fought for their meal
Of bread and snow.

Small beaks prodded;
Brown wings flickered;
To the last morsel
They tugged and bickered.

Then all in twilight,
Their feasting done,
They perched on a nut-tree
Every one,

Waiting the signal.
Suddenly – whoosh! –
To evergreen thicket
And ivy-bush

They were gone for the night ...
But one bird came
With tiny claw
To the window-frame,

Clinging and fluttering
A moment there;
Oh, take him in
From the cold air!

The Blackbird

She builds her nest on a bare branch,
In reaching-distance from the ground,
And hopes the loosening hawthorn-buds
With their quick leaves will wrap her round.

Look, down she drops to the pasture-field,
Tussling for grass in the hard earth!
Now back to her nest again. Her time
Is on her: her eggs cry out for birth.

But soon an April storm blows up –
Three nights and days of freezing air.
Leafing's delayed. Sulky she sits,
Plain to all eyes, exposed and bare.

Then comes a boy's rough hand. Then she,
Pushed out, and hopelessly looking on,
Sees with sharp eyes her hard-won nest
Battered, her shining children gone.

The Vixen

On these dark nights
The vixen stirs
From her sandy den
Beneath the firs,

And over the turf
Glides softly down
To the nearest streets
Of the quiet town.

Along the pavement,
Between the rows
Of silent houses! –
And as she goes

Her strong fox-scent
Comes first on the air,
And warns all creatures
That danger's near.

In the hushed back-gardens
The small cats flee
With desperate claws
To the nearest tree,

To lie all night
Aloft in the dark;
The chained dog wakens:
His clamorous bark

Comes echoing back
From the near hill;
In her hutch, the rabbit
Quakes, and is still.

But she, the vixen,
Desperate for food,
Risking her life
For her soft brood,

Routs round for savoury
Morsels, hid
Beneath upturned can,
And dustbin-lid.

With ears and nostrils
Tensely awake,
She gorges full,
For her cubs' sake.

Then off and away
Up the turfy slope,
To the clump of trees
On the dark hill-top,

Where she noses in
To her secret lair,
And finds her corner,
And settles down there.

Her five cubs rouse
At the scent of her,
And come snuggling close
To her warm fur.

For a while they whimper,
As small cubs will,
And fidget and fight
For a place, until –

A long and satisfied
Stillness creeps
Over them all:
They feed – she sleeps.

The Lone Pilot

Sometimes at night,
When the wind rages round about
And seems to shake the sky,
A plane comes cruising high,
With faintly-moving light
And distant drone ...

On winter nights, and I in my bed alone.

I watch that single spark
Move slowly westward into the dark,
And all my thoughts reach out
To the one man there
Who rides the sky, cushioned by clouds and air.

Who, as he rolls
Along the drowsy miles,
Must watch the lighted dials,
Straining his ears for voice or bleep;
And must still keep
Firm hands on the controls,
And never dare to close his eyes in sleep.

Good Friday

How good to be once more in bed!
Smooth sheets, and coverlet of pink and grey!
To spread
Tired limbs and turn my thoughts upon
The things of the day!

All a long morning clear and fine
We worked, father and I, with garden hoe
And line,
To set the first seeds of the year,
Row upon row.

'No meals today!' And laughingly
Mother brought out a tray with buttered bun
And tea;
While Simpkin nosed the fence, and found
A place in the sun.

All afternoon we worked to trim
The lawns, while father joked and Mother smiled
On him.
I moved between them, almost wanting
No other child.

Quietly at tea we sat; the clear
Flames crackled up from a fire of sticks and coal;
And near
My plate the yellow fluff-catkins stood
In their green bowl.

Now bed at last, with a warm drink ...
Lying so curled, and hearing, as I lie,
The clink
Of cups as Mother rinses them
And puts them by;

With sounds from out-of-doors half-heard:
Voices; a starting car; the tiny cheep
Of a bird.
I do not think it will be long
Before I sleep.

The Christmas Tree

They chopped her down in some far wood
A week ago,
Shook from her dark green spikes her load
Of gathered snow,
And brought her home at last, to be
Our Christmas show.

A week she shone, sprinkled with lamps
And fairy frost;
Now, with her boughs all stripped, her lights
And spangles lost,
Out in the garden there, leaning
On a broken post,

She sighs gently . . . Can it be
She longs to go
Back to that far-off wood, where green
And wild things grow?
Back to her dark green sisters, standing
In wind and snow?

Ann's Flowers

Ann with hot fingers grasped her flowers
    A long half-day.
'See, they are withering, Ann; you'd best
    Throw them away.'

Yet still through lane and by-way on
    And on she trailed,
Till scent of flowers was one with warmth
    Of hand that held.

But when she knew that water now
    Would never bring
Freshness, she found a bank, with moss
    For covering;

There, lulled by reeds of grass and cooled
    By shade of tree,
A bed she made, in which they could
    Die quietly.

Taking Out Jim

We left the dusty
Road and wheeled
The push-chair straight
Into the field;
So thick the dande-
lions grew,
We thought we'd deck
The baby too.

So standing in
A circle round him,
With Linda's straw
School-hat we crowned him;
Stuck dandelions
Round the band,
And squeezed a big one
In his hand.

With dandelion-
Chains a-swinging,
We sang his praise
In softest singing;
We called him Dande-
-lion Jim,
And pelted him,
And tickled him.

Half-smothered under
Linda's hat,
All giggling
And plump he sat,

A pollen-patch
Upon his nose,
And juice-stains down
His new white blouse.

Then, overcome
By sudden fears,
We brushed the petals
From his ears,
Straightened his hair
With Beryl's comb,
And thought we'd better
Take him home.

Index of First Lines